B E P A T I

Be Patient

WARREN W. WIERSBE

While this book is intended for the reader's personal enjoyment and profit, it is also designed for group study. A leader's guide with Reproducible Response Sheets is available from your local bookstore or from the publisher.

VICTOR BOOKS®

A DIVISION OF SCRIPTURE PRESS PUBLICATIONS INC.
USA CANADA ENGLAND

Library of Congress Cataloging-in-Publication Data

Wiersbe, Warren W.
    Be patient / Warren W. Wiersbe.
       p.   cm.
    ISBN 0-89693-896-4
    1. Bible. O.T. Job—Criticism, interpretation, etc.   I. Title.
    BS1415.2.W52 1991
    223'.107—dc20   91-20341
                                             CIP

1 2 3 4 5 6 7 8 9 10 Printing/Year 95 94 93 92 91

CONTENTS

Dedicated with deep appreciation
to our "prayer partners"
(you know who you are)
whose prayer support and
encouragement have been greatly
used of God.

"We thank our God upon every
remembrance of you."

And we are praying for you!

PREFACE

"You have heard of the patience [endurance] of Job" (James 5:11).

Yes, many people have *heard* about Job and his trials; but not many people *understand* what those trials were all about and what God was trying to accomplish. Nor do they realize that Job suffered as he did so that God's people today might learn from his experiences how to be patient in suffering and endure to the end.

When I decided to write about Job, I said to my wife, "I wonder how much suffering we'll have to go through so I can write this book." (I don't want to write or preach in an impersonal and academic way. The Word has to become real to me, or I can't make it real to others.) Little did we realize the trials that God would permit us to experience! But we can testify that God is faithful, He answers prayer, and He always has a wonderful purpose in mind (Jer. 29:11).

You too may have to go through the furnace in order to study the Book of Job and really grasp its message. If so, don't be afraid! By faith, just say with Job, "But He knows the way that I take; when He has tested me, I will come forth as gold" (Job 23:10, NIV). Gold fears no fire. Whatever we have that is burned up and left behind in the furnace wasn't worth having anyway.

As we study the Book of Job together, I trust that two things will be accomplished in your life: you will learn to be patient in your own trials, and you will learn how to help others in their trials. Your world is filled with people who need encouragement, and God may be preparing you for just that ministry. Either way, I hope this book helps you.

Warren W. Wiersbe

A Suggested Outline of the Book of Job

I. Job's Distress—1–3
   1. His Prosperity—1:1-5
   2. His Adversity—1:6–2:13
     loss of wealth—family—health
   3. His Perplexity—3:1-26

II. Job's Defense—4–37
   1. The First Round—4–14
     a. Eliphaz—4–5—Job's reply, 6–7
     b. Bildad—8—Job's reply, 9–10
     c. Zophar—11—Job's reply, 12–14
   2. The Second Round—15–21
     a. Eliphaz—15—Job's reply, 16–17
     b. Bildad—18—Job's reply, 19–20
     c. Zophar—20—Job's reply, 21
   3. The Third Round—22–37
     a. Eliphaz—22—Job's reply, 23–24
     b. Bildad—25—Job's reply, 26–31
     c. Elihu—32–37

III. Job's Deliverance—38–42
   1. God Humbles Job—38:1–42:6
     (see 40:3-5 and 42:1-6)
   2. God Honors Job—42:7-17
     a. God rebukes his critics—42:7-10
     b. God restores his wealth—42:11-17

"Trust the past to the mercy of God, the present to His love, and the future to His providence."

St. Augustine

The Drama Begins

L ord Byron was on target when he wrote: "Truth is always strange; stranger than fiction."

The Book of Job is not religious fiction. Job was a real person, not an imaginary character; both Ezekiel (14:14, 20) and James (5:11) attest to that. Because he was a real man who had real experiences, he can tell us what we need to know about life and its problems in this real world.

These first three chapters introduce us to the man Job and reveal four important facts about him.

1. Job's prosperity (Job 1:1-5)

The land of Uz was probably in or near Edom (Lam. 4:21). Eliphaz, one of Job's friends, came from Teman, which is associated with the Edomites (Job 2:11; Gen. 36:11).

His character (Job 1:1). Job was "perfect and upright" (Job 1:1). He was not sinless, for nobody can claim that distinction; but he was complete and mature in character and "straight" in conduct. The word translated "perfect" is related to "integrity," another important word in Job (2:3, 9; 27:5; 31:6). People with integrity are whole persons, without hypocrisy or duplicity. In the face of his friends' accusations and

God's silence, Job maintained his integrity; and the Lord ultimately vindicated him.

The foundation for Job's character was the fact that he "feared God and shunned evil." "Behold, the fear of the Lord, that is wisdom; and to depart from evil is understanding" (28:28). To fear the Lord means to respect who He is, what He says, and what He does. It is not the cringing fear of a slave before a master but the loving reverence of a child before a father, a respect that leads to obedience. "The remarkable thing about fearing God," said Oswald Chambers, "is that when you fear God you fear nothing else, whereas if you do not fear God you fear everything else."

His family (Job 1:2). Job was prosperous in his family. The events in Job took place during the Patriarchal Age when a large family was seen as a blessing from God (Gen. 12:2; 13:16; 30:1). The children must have enjoyed each other's company since they met frequently to celebrate their birthdays. This speaks well of the way Job and his wife raised them. The fact that their father offered special sacrifices after each birthday feast does not prove their celebration was wicked. It only shows that Job was a pious man and wanted to be sure his family was right with God.

His material possessions (Job 1:3). In those days, wealth was measured primarily in terms of land, animals, and servants; and Job had all three in abundance. But being rich did not turn him away from God. He acknowledged that the Lord gave this wealth to him (Job 1:21), and he used his wealth generously for the good of others (4:1-4; 29:12-17; 31:16-32). Job would have had no problem obeying what Paul wrote in 1 Timothy 6:6-19.

His friends (Job 2:11). While it is true that his three friends hurt Job deeply and wronged him greatly, they were still his friends. When they heard about Job's calamities, they traveled a long distance to visit him; and they sat in silence as they sympathized with him. Their mistake was in thinking they had to explain Job's situation and tell him how to change it.

"My best friend," said Henry Ford, "is the one who brings out the best in me"; but Job's friends brought out the worst in him. However, in the end Job and his friends were reconciled (42:7-10); and I like to think that their relationship was deeper than before. To have true friends is to be wealthy indeed.

2. Job's adversity (Job 1:6-19)

In one day, Job was stripped of his wealth. One after another, four frightened messengers reported that 500 yoke of oxen, 500 donkeys, and 3,000 camels were stolen in enemy raids; 7,000 sheep were struck by lightning and killed; and all 10 of his children were killed by a windstorm. King Solomon was right: "Moreover, no man knows when his hour will come: As fish are caught in a cruel net, or birds are taken in a snare, so men are trapped by evil times that fall unexpectedly upon them" (Ecc. 9:12, NIV).

Job knew *what* had happened, but he did not know *why* it had happened; and that is the crux of the matter. Because the author allows us to visit the throne room of heaven and hear God and Satan speak, we know who caused the destruction and why he was allowed to cause it. But if we did not have this insight, we would probably take the same approach as Job's friends and blame Job for the tragedy.

Several important truths emerge from this scene, not the least of which is that *God is sovereign in all things.* He is on the throne of heaven, the angels do His will and report to Him, and even Satan can do nothing to God's people without God's permission. "The Almighty" is one of the key names for God in Job; it is used thirty-one times. From the outset, the writer reminds us that, no matter what happens in this world and in our lives, God is on the throne and has everything under control.

A second truth—and it may surprise you—is that *Satan has access to God's throne in heaven.* Thanks to John Milton's *Paradise Lost,* many people have the mistaken idea that Satan is ruling this world from hell ("Better to reign in hell, than serve in heav'n"). But Satan will not be cast into the lake of fire until before the final judgment (Rev. 20:10ff). Today, he is free to go about *on the earth* (Job 1:7; 1 Peter 5:8) and can even go into God's presence in heaven.

This third truth is most important: *God found no fault with Job, but Satan did.* God's statement in Job 1:8 echoes the description of Job in verse 1, but Satan questioned it. The word "Satan" means "adversary, one who opposes the law." This is a courtroom scene, and God and Satan each deliver different verdicts about Job. As you study this book, keep in mind that God said "Not guilty!" (1:8; 2:3; 42:7) There was nothing in Job's life that compelled God to cause him to suffer. But Satan said "Guilty!" because he is the accuser of God's people and finds nothing good in them (Zech. 3; Rev. 12:10).

Satan's accusation against Job was really an attack on God. We might paraphrase it like this: "The only reason Job fears You is because You pay him to do it. You two have made a contract: You protect him and prosper him as long as he obeys You and worships You. You are not a God worthy of worship! You have to pay people to honor You."

Job's three friends said Job was suffering because he had sinned, and that was not true. Elihu said that God was chastening Job to make him a better man, and that was partly true. But the fundamental reason for Job's suffering was *to silence the blasphemous accusations of Satan and prove that a man would honor God even though he had lost everything.* It was a battle "in the heavenlies" (Eph. 6:12), but Job did not know it. Job's life was a battlefield where the forces of God and Satan were engaged in a spiritual struggle to decide the question, "Is Jehovah God worthy of man's worship?"

Now we can better understand why Job was so unyielding as he resisted the advice of his friends. They wanted him to repent of his sins so that God would remove the suffering and make him prosperous again. Job was not going to "invent" sin in his life just so he could repent and "earn" the blessing of God. *To do that would be to play right into the hands of the accuser!* Instead, Job held fast to his integrity and blessed God even though he did not understand what God was doing. What a defeat for the prince of darkness!

A fourth truth emerges: *Satan can touch God's people only with God's permission, and God uses it for their good and His glory.* Phillips Brooks said, "The purpose of life is the building of character through truth." God is at work in our lives to make us more like Jesus Christ (Rom. 8:29), and He can use even the attacks of the devil to perfect us. When you are in the path of obedience and you find yourself in a severe trial, remind yourself that nothing can come to your life that is outside His will.

Some of the so-called tragedies in the lives of God's people have really been weapons of God to "still the enemy and the avenger" (Ps. 8:2). The angels watch the church and learn from God's dealings with His people (1 Cor. 4:9; Eph. 3:10). We may not know until we get to heaven why God allowed certain things to happen. Meanwhile, we walk by faith and say with Job, "Blessed be the name of the Lord."

3. Job's fidelity (Job 1:20-22)
The hosts of heaven and of hell watched to see how Job would respond to the loss of his wealth and his children. He expressed his grief in a manner normal for that day, for God expects us to be human (1 Thes. 4:13). After all, even Jesus

wept (John 11:35). But then Job worshiped God and uttered a profound statement of faith (Job 1:21).

First, he *looked back* to his birth: "Naked came I out of my mother's womb." Everything Job owned was given to him by God, and the same God who gave it had the right to take it away. Job simply acknowledged that he was a steward.

Then Job *looked ahead* to his death: "and naked shall I return." He would not return to his mother's womb, because that would be impossible. He would go to "Mother Earth," be buried, and turn to dust. (The connection between "birth" and "Mother Earth" is seen also in Ps. 139:13-15.) Nothing that he acquired between his birth and death would go with him into the next world. Paul wrote, "For we brought nothing into this world, and it is certain we can carry nothing out" (1 Tim. 6:7).

Finally, Job *looked up* and uttered a magnificent statement of faith: "The Lord gave, and the Lord hath taken away; blessed be the name of the Lord" (Job 1:21). Instead of cursing God, as Satan said Job would do, Job blessed the Lord! Anybody can say, "The Lord gave" or "The Lord hath taken away"; but it takes real faith to say in the midst of sorrow and suffering, "Blessed be the name of the Lord."

"In all this Job sinned not, nor charged God with folly" (v. 22).

4. Job's misery (Job 2:1–3:26)

In this section, you hear four different voices.

The voice of the accuser (Job 2:1-8). Satan does not give up easily, for he returned to God's throne to accuse Job again. As in the first meeting (1:8), it is God who brings up the subject of His servant Job; and Satan accepts the challenge. We get the impression that God is confident His servant will not fail the test.

"Every man has his price," said Satan. "Job can raise an-

18

other family and start another business because he still has health and strength. Let me touch his body and take away his health, and You will soon hear him curse You to Your face."

With God's permission (1 Cor. 10:13), Satan afflicted Job with a disease we cannot identify. Whatever it was, the symptoms were terrible: severe itching (Job 2:8), insomnia (v. 4), running sores and scabs (v. 5), nightmares (vv. 13-14), bad breath (19:17), weight loss (v. 20), chills and fever (21:6), diarrhea (30:27), and blackened skin (v. 30). When his three friends first saw Job, they did not recognize him! (2:12)

Not all physical affliction comes directly from the evil one, though Satan's demons can cause (among other things) blindness (Matt. 12:22), dumbness (9:32-33), physical deformities (Luke 13:11-17), incessant pain (2 Cor. 12:7), and insanity (Matt. 8:28-34). Sometimes physical affliction is the natural result of carelessness on our part, and we have nobody to blame but ourselves. But even then, Satan knows how to use our folly to further his cause.

So abhorrent was Job's appearance that he fled society (Job 19:13-20) and went outside the city and sat on the ash heap. There the city garbage was deposited and burned, and there the city's rejects lived, begging alms from whoever passed by. At the ash heap, dogs fought over something to eat, and the city's dung was brought and burned. The city's leading citizen was now living in abject poverty and shame.

The voice of the quitter (Job 2:9-10). If ever a believer in Old Testament days shared in the fellowship of Christ's sufferings, it was Job. All that he humanly had left was his wife and his three friends, and even they turned against him. No wonder Job felt that God had deserted him!

"Curse God and die!" was exactly what Satan wanted Job to do, and Job's wife put the temptation before her husband. Yes, Satan can work through people who are dear to us (Matt. 16:22-23; Acts 21:10-14); and the temptation is stronger because we love them so much. Adam listened to Eve (Gen. 3:6, 12), and Abraham listened to Sarah (Gen. 16); but Job did not listen to the advice of his wife.

She was wrong, of course; but in all fairness, we must consider her situation. She had lost ten children in one day, and that would be enough to devastate any mother. The family wealth was gone, and she was no longer the "leading lady" in the land. Her husband, once the greatest man in the East (Job 1:3), was now sitting at the city garbage dump, suffering from a terrible disease. What did she have left? Rather than watch her husband waste away in pain and shame, she would prefer that God strike him dead and get it over with immediately. Perhaps if Job cursed God, God would do it.

In times of severe testing, our first question must not be, *"How* can I get out of this?" but *"What* can I get out of this?" Job's wife thought she had the problem solved; but if Job had followed her counsel, it would have only made things worse. Faith is living without scheming. It is obeying God in spite of feelings, circumstances, or consequences, knowing that He is working out His perfect plan in His way and in His time.

The two things Job would not give up were his faith in God and his integrity, and that's what his wife wanted him to do. Even if God did permit evil to come into his life, Job would not rebel against God by taking matters into his own hands. Job had never read *The Letters of Samuel Rutherford*, but he was following the counsel of that godly Scottish pastor who suffered greatly: "It is faith's work to claim and challenge loving-kindness out of all the roughest strokes of God." Job was going to trust God—and even argue with God!—and not waste his sufferings or his opportunity to receive what God had for him.

When life is difficult, it's easy to give up; but giving up is the worst thing we can do. A professor of history said, "If

20

Columbus had turned back, nobody would have blamed him—but nobody would have remembered him either." If you want to be memorable, sometimes you have to be miserable.

In the end, Job's wife was reconciled to her husband and to the Lord, and God gave her another family (42:13). We don't know how much she learned from her sufferings; but we can assume it was a growing experience for her.

The voice of the mourners (Job 2:11-13). The term "Job's comforters" is a familiar phrase for describing people whose help only makes you feel worse. But these three men had some admirable qualities in spite of the way they persecuted Job.

For one thing, they cared enough for Job to travel a long distance to visit him. And when they commiserated with him, they didn't sit in a comfortable home or hospital room: they sat with him on the ash heap, surrounded by refuse. Because their grief was so great, they couldn't speak for seven days. (Of course, they made up for their silence afterward.) In fact, their expression of grief was like mourning for the death of a great person (Gen. 50:10).

The best way to help people who are hurting is just to be with them, saying little or nothing, and letting them know you care. Don't try to explain everything; explanations never heal a broken heart. If his friends had listened to him, accepted his feelings, and not argued with him, they would have helped him greatly; but they chose to be prosecuting attorneys instead of witnesses. In the end, the Lord rebuked them; and they had to ask Job's forgiveness (Job 42:7-10).

The voice of the sufferer (Job 3:1-26). After seven days of silent suffering, Job spoke, not to curse God but to curse the day of his birth. "Why was I ever born?" has been sobbed by more than one hurting child of God, including the Prophet Jeremiah (Jer. 20:14-18). This is not quite the same as saying, "I wish I were dead"; though Job did express that desire more than once (Job 6:9; 7:15-16; 14:13). *At no time did Job speak of ending his own life.* Job's "birthday lament" is not a defense of suicide or so-called "mercy killing." It is the declaration of a man whose suffering was so intense that he wished he had never been born.

When you are hurting, you may say and do a lot of things that you later regret. Job's suffering was so great that he forgot the blessings that he and his family had enjoyed for so many years. Had he never been born, he would never have been the greatest man in the East! But pain makes us forget the joys of the past; instead, we concentrate on the hopelessness of the future. Job's friends heard his words but did not feel the anguish of his heart, and they took the wrong approach to helping him handle his trials. They argued with his words instead of ministering to his feelings.

Job cursed two nights: the night of his conception and the night of his birth (3:1-13). Conception is a blessing that comes from God (Gen. 30:1-2; Ps. 139:13-16); so when we curse a blessing, we are questioning the goodness of God. (Note that Job said a *child* was conceived, not "a mass of protoplasm" or "a thing." He was a *person* from conception.)

The key word here is *darkness.* When a baby is born, it comes out of darkness into the light; but Job wanted to stay in the darkness. In fact, he thought it would have been better if he had been born dead! Then he would have gone to the world of the dead (Sheol) and not had to face all this misery.

He closed his curse with four "why?" questions that nobody but God could answer. It is easy to ask why but difficult to get the right answer. There is nothing wrong with asking why, as long as we don't get the idea that God *owes* us an answer. Even our Lord asked, "Why hast Thou forsaken Me?" (Matt. 27:46) But if the Lord did tell us why things happen as they do, would that ease our pain or heal our broken hearts? Does reading the X ray take away the pain of a broken leg? We live on *promises*, not explanations; so we shouldn't spend too much time asking God why.

The last half of the lament is a description of the world of the dead, the place the Jews called Sheol (Job 3:13-26). That's where Job wanted to be! The Old Testament does not give a complete and final revelation of life after death; that had to await the coming of the Savior (2 Tim. 1:10). Job saw Sheol as a shadowy place where the small and great rested together, away from the burdens and sufferings of life on earth. Job would rather be dead and have rest than be alive and bear the misery that had come to him. After all, he was in the dark as far as his future was concerned (Job 3:23), so he might as well be in the darkness of Sheol.

Job shares a secret at the close of his lament (vv. 25-26): before all his troubles started, he had a feeling—and a fear—that something terrible was going to happen. Was it an intuition from the Lord? Sometimes God's people have these intuitions, and it motivates them to seek God's face and pray for His help. Is that what Job did? We don't know, but we do know that he was a broken man whose worst fears had now been realized.

It is unfortunate that the three friends laid hold of Job's lament instead of his statement of faith (1:21; 2:10). After hearing him curse his birthday, they felt it necessary to rebuke him and come to God's defense.

Now the discussion begins. Soon it will become a debate, then a dispute; and the Lord will have to intervene to bring matters to a head.

INTERLUDE

You will be spending a good deal of time with Job's three friends, so you had better get acquainted with them.

All three of the men were old (Job 32:6), older than Job (15:10), but we assume that *Eliphaz* was the oldest. He is named first (2:11), he spoke first, and the Lord seems to have accepted him as the elder member of the trio (42:7). He was associated with Teman, a place known for its wisdom (Jer. 49:7). Eliphaz based his speeches on two things: his own observations of life ("I have seen"—Job 4:8; 5:3, 27, NASB), and a frightening personal experience he had one night (4:12-21). Eliphaz put great faith in tradition (15:18-19), and the God he worshiped was an inflexible Lawgiver. "Who ever perished being innocent?" he asked (4:7); and a host of martyrs could have answered, "We have!" (And what about our Lord Jesus Christ?) Eliphaz had a rigid theology that left little or no room for the grace of God.

Bildad must have been the second oldest of the three since he is named second and spoke after Eliphaz. In a word, Bildad was a *legalist.* His life-text was, "Behold, God will not cast away a perfect man, neither will He help the evildoers" (8:20). He could quote ancient proverbs and, like Eliphaz, he had great respect for tradition. For some reason, Bildad was sure that Job's children died because they also were sinners (v. 4). The man seemed to have no feeling for his hurting friend.

Zophar was the youngest of the three and surely the most dogmatic. He speaks like a schoolmaster addressing a group of ignorant freshmen. "Know this!" is his unfeeling approach (11:6; 20:4). He is merciless and tells Job that God was giving him far less than he deserved for his sins! (11:6) His key text is, "Knowest thou not this of old ... that the triumphing of the wicked is short, and the joy of the hypocrite but for a moment?" (20:4-5) Interestingly enough, Zophar speaks to Job only twice. Either he decided he was unable to answer Job's arguments or felt that it was a waste of time trying to help Job.

All three men said some good and true things, as well as some foolish things; but they were of no help to Job because their viewpoint was too narrow. Their theology was not vital and vibrant but dead and rigid, and the God they tried to defend was small enough to be understood and explained. These men perfectly illustrate Dorothy Sayers' statement, "There's nothing you can't prove if your outlook is only sufficiently limited."

Why would three men speak to their friend as these men spoke to Job? Why were they so angry? There is a hint of an answer in Job's words, "Now you too have proved to be of no help; you see something dreadful and are afraid" (6:21, NIV). *The three men were afraid that the same calamities would come to them!* Therefore, they had to defend their basic premise that God rewards the righteous and punishes the wicked. As long as they were "righteous," nothing evil could happen to them in this life.

Fear and anger often go together. By maintaining his integrity and refusing to say he had sinned, Job undermined the theology of his friends and robbed them of their peace and confidence; and this made them angry. God used Job to destroy their shallow theology and challenge them to go deeper into the heart and mind of God. Alas, they preferred the superficial and safe to the profound and mysterious.

Eliphaz, Bildad, and Zophar have many disciples today. Whenever you meet a person who feels compelled to explain everything, who has a pat answer for every question and a fixed formula for solving every problem, you are back at the ash heap with Job's three friends. When that happens, remember the words of the Swiss psychologist, Paul Tournier:

> We are nearly always longing for an easy religion, easy to understand and easy to follow; a religion with no mystery, no insoluble problems, no snags; a religion that would allow us to escape from our miserable human condition; a religion in which contact with God spares us all strife, all uncertainty, all suffering and all doubt; in short, a religion without the Cross.
> (*Reflections* [New York: Harper & Row, 1976], 142)

We wonder how Job's three friends would have explained the Cross to the two Emmaus disciples! (Luke 24:13ff) Now, let's listen in on the first round of speeches.

"But what Satan could not do with all his Sabeans, and all his Chaldeans, and all his winds from the wilderness to help him, that he soon did with the debating approaches and the controversial assaults of Eliphaz, and Zophar, and Bildad, and Elihu. Oh, the unmitigable curse of controversy!"

Alexander Whyte

The Discussion Begins

The three friends were silent for seven days (Job 2:13), and Job later wished they had stayed that way (13:5). "Then Eliphaz, the Temanite, answered [Job]." But what did he answer? The pain in Job's heart? No, he answered the words from Job's lips; *and this was a mistake.* A wise counselor and comforter must listen with the heart and respond to feelings as well as to words. You do not heal a broken heart with logic; you heal a broken heart with love. Yes, you must speak the truth; but be sure to speak the truth in love (Eph. 4:15).

1. Eliphaz's rebuke (Job 4-5)

His approach (Job 4:1-4). Eliphaz's approach seems to start out positive enough, even gentle; but it was only honey to prepare Job for the bitterness that would follow. "If someone ventures a word with you, will you be impatient?" he asked (v. 2, NIV).

"Don't get upset, Job!" is what he was saying. "In the past, your words have been a help to many people; and we want our words to be a help to you."

Never underestimate the power of words to encourage

27

people in the battles of life. James Moffatt translates Job 4:4, "Your words have kept men on their feet." The right words, spoken at the right time, and with the right motive, can make a tremendous difference in the lives of others. Your words can nourish those who are weak and encourage those who are defeated. But your words can also hurt those who are broken and only add to their burdens, so be careful what you say and how you say it.

His accusation (Job 4:5-11). Eliphaz then moved into his accusation. Job could "give it," but he couldn't "take it"! He could tell others how to handle their trials; but when trials came to his life, he didn't practice what he preached. "Is not your reverence your confidence?" asked Eliphaz. "And the integrity of your ways your hope?" (v. 6, NKJV) If Job is living a godly life, Eliphaz argues, then he has nothing to fear; because God *always* blesses the righteous and judges the wicked.

This is the basic premise of all three friends: Do what is right, and things will go well for you; do what is wrong, and God will send judgment. That judgment may sometimes be gradual, like the growing of a crop for harvest (v. 8); or it may be sudden, like the coming of a storm or the attack of a lion (vv. 9-11). But you can be sure that judgment will come; for God is a righteous Judge.

Most people will agree that *ultimately* God blesses the righteous, His own people, and judges the wicked; but that is not the question discussed in Job. It is not the *ultimate* but the *immediate* about which Job and his three friends are concerned, and not only they but also David (Ps. 37), Asaph (Ps. 73), and even the Prophet Jeremiah (Jer. 12:1-6).

His arguments (Job 4:12–5:7). Eliphaz presented two arguments to prove his point: experience (4:12-21) and observation (5:1-7). The first argument is based on an eerie experience he had one night when he saw a "vision" and heard a voice. Two questions must be answered: What was the content of the message, and was the message a direct revelation from God?

Since there are no punctuation marks in the Hebrew manuscripts of the Old Testament, we are not always certain where quotations begin and end. Most English translations make 4:17-21 the complete statement of the "spirit"; but some students feel the statement is limited to verse 17, and the rest is commentary by Eliphaz. Either way, it's the same message: man's life is brief and frail, and he can never be righteous enough in himself to please God.

But was this statement a direct revelation from God? Probably not; the whole experience doesn't seem to fit God's pattern for revealing truth. For one thing, it lacks the authority of "The word of the Lord came to me saying" or "Thus says the Lord." And God doesn't usually "sneak up on" people and scare them. We don't know for sure, but it's possible that Eliphaz had a dream, meditated on it, and gradually transformed it into a vision.

One thing is sure: Eliphaz was not telling the whole story about God and man. Yes, man lives in a house of clay that eventually turns to dust; and man's life can be snuffed out like swatting a moth or pulling down a tent. But man is also made in the image of God, and the God who made him is a God of grace and mercy as well as a God of justice.

Eliphaz's second argument is based on his own personal observations of life (5:1-7). He has seen sinners prosper and take root, only to be destroyed and lose everything. This was a not-so-subtle description of Job's situation. It must have hurt Job deeply to hear that it was his sin that killed his children. But in Psalm 73, Asaph takes a wholly different view. He concludes that God allows the wicked to prosper in this life because it's the only "heaven" they will know. God will adjust things in the next life and see to it that His people are rewarded and the wicked are punished.

The problem with arguing from observation is that our observations are severely limited. Furthermore, we can't see the human heart as God can and determine who is righteous in His sight. Some sinners suffer judgment almost immediately, while others spend their lives in prosperity and die in peace (Ecc. 8:10-14).

Trouble doesn't grow out of the ground, like weeds; it's a part of man's birth, because man is born a sinner (Job 5:6-7). If Job is in trouble, concludes Eliphaz, he caused it himself because he sinned against God. Therefore, Job must repent of his sins and ask for God's forgiveness.

His appeal (Job 5:8-17). This leads to an appeal from Eliphaz that Job seek God and commit himself to Him. The God who does wonders and cares for His creation will surely help Job if he humbles himself and confesses his sins. Job should see his trials as discipline from God to make him a better man (vv. 17-18), a theme that will later be taken up by Elihu. Job must have been in bad shape for God to have to take away his wealth, his family, and his health in order to straighten him out! And isn't discipline a tool of God's love? (Prov. 3:11-12; Heb. 12:1-11)

His assurance (Job 5:17-27). Eliphaz closes his speech with words of assurance. The same God who wounds will also heal (Deut. 32:39; Hosea 6:1-2). He will deliver you from trouble, save you from your enemies, and give you a long and happy life and a peaceful death. "We have examined this, and it is true. So hear it and apply it to yourself" (Job 5:27, NIV).

But this is Satan's philosophy said in different words! "Does Job fear God for nothing? . . . Skin for skin! Yes, all that a man has he will give for his life" (1:9; 2:4, NKJV). Eliphaz was asking Job to make a bargain with God: Confess your sins, and God will restore all that you have lost. If Job had done that, it would have disgraced Jehovah and vindicated Satan; and Job was not about to do it.

2. Job's response (Job 6–7)

Job responded with two passionate appeals. First, he appealed to his three friends that they might show more understanding and sympathy (Job 6). Then he appealed to God, that He would consider his plight and lighten his sufferings before he died (Job 7).

Job's appeal to his friends (Job 6). Only Eliphaz had spoken so far, but Job could tell that Bildad and Zophar agreed with him. Not one of his friends identified with what Job was going through physically and emotionally. It was one thing for them to sit where he sat and quite something else for them to feel what he felt (Ezek. 3:15). The child who defined "sympathy" as "your pain in my heart" knew more about giving comfort than did these three.

To begin with, they didn't feel the *heaviness* of his suffering (Job 6:1-3). No wonder Job had spoken so impetuously! His friends would have done the same thing if they carried the load that he carried. Job didn't have the full revelation of heaven that believers have today, so his future was dim. We can read 2 Corinthians 4:16-18 and take heart.

Nor did his friends understand the *bitterness* of his suffering (Job 6:4-7). Job felt like a target at which God was shooting poisoned arrows, and the poison was making Job's spirit bitter. God had His army in array, shooting at one weak man; and Job's friends were adding to the poison. What Job needed were words of encouragement that would feed his spirit and give him strength, but all his friends fed him were words that were useless and tasteless. If his complaint sounded like the braying of a donkey or the lowing of an ox, it was because, like a starving animal, he was hungry for love and understanding.

Job tried to get them to feel the *hopelessness* of his situation (vv. 8-13). Prolonged and intense suffering can make a person feel powerless to handle life, and this can lead to hopelessness. If you can't control some of the elements that make up life, how can you plan for the future? Job asked, "What strength do I have, that I should still hope? What prospects, that I should be patient?" (v. 11, NIV) In other words, "What am I waiting for? Life is only getting worse!"

Hopelessness can lead to a feeling of *uselessness;* and when you feel useless, you don't want to live. This explains why Job wanted God to take his life (3:20-23; 6:8-9; 7:15-16; 10:18-19; 14:13). Job didn't attempt this himself, for he knew that suicide was wrong; but he prayed that God might take him out of his misery. Job's friends were healthy and comfortable and didn't know the burden of waking up each morning to another day of suffering. Job's strength was gone, and he felt useless (6:12-13).

Courageously, Job pointed out the *ineffectiveness* of their ministry to him (vv. 14-30). They didn't pity him or try to meet his needs. They were like a dry brook in the desert that disappoints thirsty travelers. They were his "friends" as long as he was prosperous; but when trouble came, they turned against him.

Job made two requests of his friends: "Teach me" (v. 24) and "Look upon me" (v. 28). He didn't need accusation; he needed illumination! But they wouldn't even look him in the face and behold his plight. Physically, the three men were sitting with Job on the ash heap; but emotionally, they were like the priest and Levite, passing by "on the other side" (Luke 10:30-37).

In my pastoral ministry, I can recall visiting hospital patients who were difficult to look at because of disease, accident, or surgery; and sometimes they were difficult to listen to because they had become bitter. From my eye contact and my responses to their words, they could detect whether or not I really cared. It did little good for me to quote Scripture and pray unless we had first built a bridge between our hearts. Then we could minister to each other.

Job closed his address to his friends with a passionate appeal for them to reconsider his situation and take a more loving approach. "Relent, do not be unjust; reconsider, for my integrity is at stake" (Job 6:29, NIV). The three men were so intent on defending themselves that they forgot to comfort their friend!

Job's appeal to the Lord (Job 7). Job used several vivid pictures to describe the *futility* of life. He felt like a man who had been conscripted into the army against his will (v. 1a, "appointed time" in KJV), and like a laborer (v. 1b) or a hired man waiting for sunset and his daily wages (v. 2). At least these men had something to look forward to, but Job's future was hopeless. His nights were sleepless, his days were futile (Deut. 28:67), and the Lord didn't seem to care.

He then focused on the *brevity* of life. Time was passing swiftly; so, if God were going to do anything, He had better hurry! Job's life was like the weaver's shuttle (Job 7:6), moving swiftly with the thread running out. (The phrase "cut me off" in 6:9 means "to cut a weaving from the loom." See Isa. 38:12.) Life is like a weaving, and only God can see the total pattern and when the work is finished.

Job also saw his life as a breath or a cloud, here for a brief time and then gone forever, never to return (Job 7:7-10; James 4:14). God was treating him like a dangerous monster that had to be watched every minute (Job 7:11-12). No wonder Job was bitter against God for guarding him constantly. The fact that Job referred to *Yam* ("the sea") and *Tammin* ("a whale"), two mythological characters, didn't mean he was giving his approval to the teachings of the Eastern myths. He used these two well-known characters only to illustrate his point.

There was no way Job could escape God, the "watcher of men" (v. 20, NIV, NKJV). If Job went to sleep, God frightened him in his dreams. If he was awake, he knew God's eye was upon him (10:14; 13:27; 31:4). He couldn't even swallow his spittle without God knowing about it! Why would God pay so much attention to one man? (7:17-18; Ps. 8:4)

Job closed his appeal with a request for forgiveness (Job 7:20-21). "If I have sinned, then forgive me. Why should I be a burden to You and to myself? Time is flying by swiftly, so let's settle things as soon as possible!" It was not a confession of sin, for Job still maintained his integrity; but it was an opportunity for God to deal with areas in Job's life that he knew nothing about (Ps. 19:12-14).

Then Job was silent. He had vented his pain and frustration and appealed to his friends for understanding and encouragement. Would he receive it?

Let's listen next to Bildad the Shuhite who gives a brief theological lecture on the justice of God.

T H R E E

"You may be as orthodox as the devil, and as wicked."
John Wesley

The Discussion Continues

A s the discussion continues, Bildad presents three logical arguments to prove Job is guilty; and Job counters with three painful questions to help his friends understand how perplexed and tormented he really is.

1. Three logical arguments (Job 8:1-22)

"Your words are a blustering wind!" (Job 8:2, NIV) Can you imagine a counselor saying that to a suffering individual who wanted to die? Bildad did; in fact, he used the same approach in his next speech (18:2). Job had poured out his grief and was waiting to hear a sympathetic word, but his friend said that Job's speech was just so much hot air.

There is a reason for Bildad's approach: he was so concerned about defending the justice of God that he forgot the needs of his friend. "Does God subvert judgment? Or does the Almighty pervert justice?" (8:3, NKJV) Bildad preached a sermon on God's justice, and his text was taken from the "vision" of Eliphaz: "Shall mortal man be more just than God?" (4:17) In defending God's justice, Bildad presented three logical arguments.

The character of God (Job 8:1-7). It angered Bildad that Job even thought that God would do anything wrong. Had Job forgotten what God did to sinners at the Flood, or what He did to Sodom and Gomorrah? Isn't He the holy God, and doesn't His very nature demand that He do what is right? Job was blaspheming God by questioning Him and accusing Him of wrongdoing.

While Bildad's theology was correct—God *is* just—his application of that theology was wrong. Bildad was looking at only one aspect of God's nature—His holiness and justice—and had forgotten His love, mercy, and goodness. Yes, "God is light" (1 John 1:5); but don't forget that "God is love" (4:8, 16). His love is a holy love, and His holiness is exercised in love, even when He judges sin.

How are these two attributes of God reconciled? At the Cross. When Jesus died for the sins of the world, the righteousness of God was vindicated, for sin was judged; but the love of God was demonstrated, for a Savior was provided. At Calvary, God is both "just and the Justifier" (Rom. 3:24-26). God's law said, "The soul who sins shall die" (Ezek. 18:4, 20, NKJV); and God obeyed His own law in the sacrificing of His Son on the cross. In Christ's resurrection, the grace of God triumphed over sin and death; and all who repent of their sins and trust Jesus Christ will be saved.

In Old Testament times, believers looked forward to the Cross and were saved by faith in a Savior yet to come (John 8:56; Rom. 3:25; Heb. 11). Job was a believer; therefore, his sins had been dealt with by God. Even if Job had sinned against God in some great way, God would deal with His child on the basis of grace and mercy and not justice. When we confess our sins, God forgives us because He is faithful to His promise and just toward His Son who died for those sins (1 John 1:9).

It must have pained Job deeply when Bildad said that Job's children had died because they had sinned (Job 8:4). Bildad probably thought he was encouraging Job: "Perhaps they were not killed because of *your* sins but because of their own sins. They can't change anything now, but you can; so don't wait too long!"

Bildad's appeal in verses 5-7 is another echo of Satan's philosophy. "You say you have not sinned. Then plead with God to restore your prosperity. If you were right before God, He would do great things for you. Isn't prosperity better than pain?" Little did Bildad realize that his words would come true and Job's latter end would be greater than his beginning. However, Job would end up praying, not for himself, but for Bildad and the other friends because *they* were not right with God (42:7-13).

The wisdom of the past (Job 8:8-10). Eliphaz based his thinking on observation and experience, but Bildad was a traditionalist who looked for wisdom in the past. "What do the ancients say about it?" was his key question. To be sure, we today can learn from the past. "Those who do not remember the past are condemned to relive it," wrote George Santayana. But the past must be a rudder to guide us and not an anchor to hold us back. "How the past perishes is how the future becomes," said philosopher Alfred North Whitehead.

The fact that something was said or written years ago is no guarantee it is right. As one who enjoys reading the classics, I am impressed with the fact that they contain as much folly as wisdom; and they often contradict each other. Dr. Robert Hutchins, editor of *The Great Books of the Western World,* wrote in his preface: "In a conversation that has gone on for twenty-five centuries, all dogmas and points of view appear. Here are the great errors as well as the great truths."

"Tradition" and "traditionalism" are two different things. Historian Jeroslav Pelikan expresses this difference accurately when he says, "Tradition is the living faith of the dead; traditionalism is the dead faith of the living." To Bildad, the past was a parking lot; but God wants the past to be a launching pad. We *stand* with the ancients so that we can *walk* with them and *move* toward the goals that they were seeking. This includes our knowledge of God as well as our knowledge of man and the world. As John Robinson said to the Pilgrim Fathers when they left for the New World, "The Lord has more truth yet to break forth out of His Holy Word."

Bildad did not quote from the ancients; he knew that Job was as familiar with the past as he was. But Bildad made it clear that he respected the wisdom of the ancients more than the teachings of his contemporaries. The accumulated wisdom of the ages was bound to be worth more than the words of people who were "born only yesterday." Life is too brief for us to learn all they can teach us. We are fleeting shadows, so we had better learn wisdom while we have opportunity.

The evidence in nature (Job 8:11-22). In this "wisdom poem," Bildad may have summarized some of the sayings of the ancients as he argued from the law of "cause and effect." If this law applies in nature, why not in human life as well?

Take the papyrus plant as an example: If it doesn't have water, it withers and dies (vv. 11-13). Job was withering and dying, so there had to be a cause: he was a hypocrite, and his hope was perishing.

Bildad then moved from plants to spiders (vv. 14-15). Can you lean on a spider's web and be held up securely? Of course not! No matter how confident you may be, the web will break. Job's confidence was like that: In due time, it would break, and he would fall.

The third example came from the garden: If you pull up a plant, no matter how luxuriant it may be, it will eventually die (vv. 16-22). Something had happened to Job's "root system," and he was fading away; thus, sin was the cause. Nobody pulls up a *good* plant and destroys it, so there had to be something wrong with Job for God to so uproot him. God doesn't cultivate weeds and cast away the good plants! Bildad reaffirmed his earlier promise that God would restore Job's fortunes if he would only admit his sins and get right with God. It was the devil's invitation all over again!

2. Three painful questions (Job 9:1–10:22)

From this point on, the emphasis in the discussion is on *the justice of God;* and the image that is uppermost in Job's mind is that of *a legal trial.* He wants to take God to court and have opportunity to prove his own integrity. A glance at some of the vocabulary indicates this:

> *contend* (Job 9:3; 10:2) = enter into litigation
> *answer* (9:3, 16) = testify in court
> *judge* (v. 15) = an opponent at law, accuser
> *set a time* (v. 19) = summon to court
> *daysman* (v. 33) = an umpire, an arbitrator
> *reason* (13:3) = argue a case
> *order my cause* (v. 18) = prepare my case
> *plead* (v. 19; 23:6) = dispute in court
> *hear me* (31:35) = give me a legal hearing
> *adversary* (v. 35) = accuser in court

In Job 9 and 10, Job asks three questions: (1) "How can I be righteous before God?" (9:1-13) (2) "How can I meet God in court?" (vv. 14-35) and (3) "Why was I born?" (10:1-22; see v. 18) You can see how these questions connect. Job is righteous, but he has to prove it. How can a mortal man prove himself righteous before God? Can he take God to court? But if God doesn't step in and testify on Job's behalf, what is the purpose of all this suffering? Why was Job even born?

"How can I be righteous before God?" (Job 9:1-13) This is not a question about salvation ("How may I be justified?") but about vindication ("How can I be declared innocent?"). If

a man tried to take God to court, he would not be able to answer God's questions one time in a thousand! Yet Job doesn't know any other way to clear himself before his friends.

Most of this section is a declaration focusing on the attributes of God, especially His invincible wisdom and power that control the earth and the heavens. Would anybody dare go to court with an opponent powerful enough to shake the earth, make the stars, and walk on the waves? (See Isa. 44:24 and Amos 4:13.)

But God is not only invincible, He is also *invisible*. Job couldn't see Him or stop him to give Him a summons to court. God can do whatever He pleases, and nobody can question Him! Even the monster *Rahab* (Job 9:13, NIV, another mythological creature like *Yam* and *Tannin,* 7:12) has to bow before God's power.

"How can I meet God in court?" (Job 9:14-35) In order to prove himself righteous, Job had to take God to court. But suppose God accepted the summons? What would Job say or do? He discusses this by imagining several situations.

(1) "If God came, what would I say?" (vv. 14-19) How could Job answer God's cross-examination? How does one reason with God or present one's case before God? If God should answer, Job would not believe it was really His voice; and if Job should say the wrong thing, God would only afflict him more. When Job finally did meet God (Job 38–41), the Lord asked him seventy-seven questions! And Job couldn't answer one of them! His only response was to admit his ignorance and shut his mouth in silence.

(2) "If I could declare my innocence, what then?" (vv. 20-24) This is no assurance that God will set Job free. Both Eliphaz and Bildad claimed that God rewards the righteous and judges the wicked, but Job said that sometimes God destroys both the righteous and the wicked. Wicked judges condemn the

righteous and help the ungodly, and God apparently does nothing about it. Job is accusing God of injustice, not only toward Job and his family but also toward other innocent people in the land.

(3) "If I try to be happy, what good will it do?" (vv. 25-31) Time was running out for Job, like the king's messengers that hasten to their destinations, and the papyrus boats in Egypt that skim swiftly down the river, and the eagle that swoops down from the sky. Perhaps Job should take a more positive attitude toward his afflictions, forget his pain, and smile (v. 27). But would that change anything? No! He would still be guilty before God, rejected by his friends, and sitting on an ash heap in sickness and pain. Even if he took a bath and changed clothes as an act of public contrition and cleansing, he would still fear what God might do. Job is convinced that God is against him and that any steps he takes on earth will be nullified by heaven. The defendant can smile and put on a brave front in court, but that doesn't keep the judge from saying, "Guilty!"

(4) "If only I had a mediator!" (vv. 32-35) If God were a man, then Job could approach him and plead his case. Or if there were a "daysman" (mediator) between God and Job, he could take away the rod of judgment and bring Job and God together. But God is not man, and there is no mediator! *This is where Jesus Christ enters the picture!* Jesus is God and became man to reveal the Father (John 14:7-11) and to bring sinners to God (1 Tim. 2:5-6; 1 Peter 3:18). He is the "daysman" that Job was pleading for centuries ago (Job. 16:21).

"Why was I born?" (Job 10:1-22) Job's argument here is that God made him and gave him life (vv. 3, 8-12, 18-19), but God was not treating him like one of His own creations. After putting time and effort into making Job, God was destroying him! Furthermore, God was judging Job without even telling him what the charges were against him (v. 2). No wonder Job

was weary, bitter, and confused (vv. 1, 15). Note that in this chapter Job speaks directly to God and not to his friends.

God is not a man that He has to investigate things and fight against time (vv. 4-6). God is eternal and can take all the time He needs, and God is all-knowing and doesn't have to investigate like a private detective. Job had previously yearned for an umpire (9:33), but now he asks for a deliverer (10:7) so he can escape judgment. God was an ever-present Guard, watching Job's every move (v. 14). He was stalking Job like a lion (v. 16) and attacking him with His army (v. 17). Job was hemmed in, and there was no way out.

So Job's question seems reasonable: "Why then did You bring me out of the womb?" (v. 18, NIV) Job's existence on the earth seemed so purposeless he begged God to give him a few moments of peace and happiness before his life ended. He could see his life going by swiftly (7:6-7; 9:25-26), and there was not a moment to waste. "Let me alone," he prays, "so that I can have a little comfort before I go to the world of darkness."

Job could not understand what God was doing, *and it was important that he not understand.* Had Job known that God was using him as a weapon to defeat Satan, he could have simply sat back and waited trustfully for the battle to end. But as Job surveyed himself and his situation, he asked the same question the disciples asked when Mary anointed the Lord Jesus: "Why this waste?" (Mark 14:4) Before we criticize Job too severely, let's recall how many times we have asked that question ourselves when a baby has died or a promising young person was killed in an accident.

Nothing that is given to Christ in faith and love is ever wasted. The fragrance of Mary's ointment faded from the scene centuries ago, but the significance of her worship has blessed Christians in every age and continues to do so. Job was bankrupt and sick, and all he could give to the Lord was his suffering by faith; *but that is just what God wanted in order to silence the devil.*

When William Whiting Borden died in Egypt in 1913 while on his way to the mission field, some people may have asked, "Why this waste?" But God is still using the story of his brief life to challenge people to give Christ their all.

When John and Betty Stam were martyred in China in 1934, there were some who asked, "Why this waste?" But *The Triumph of John and Betty Stam* by Mrs. Howard Taylor has been a life-changing book since it was published in 1935. My girlfriend (now my wife) gave me a copy on my twenty-first birthday, and its message still grips my heart.

When the five missionaries were martyred in Ecuador at the hands of Auca Indians, some called the event a "tragic waste of manpower." But God thought differently, and the story of these five heroes of faith has been ministering to the church ever since.

Job asked, "Why was I born?" In the light of his losses and his personal suffering, it all seemed such a waste! But God knew what He was doing *then*, and He knows what He is doing *now*.

"You have heard of Job's perseverance and have seen what the Lord finally brought about," wrote James. "The Lord is full of compassion and mercy" (James 5:11, NIV). If you had told that to Job, he might not have believed it; but it was still true.

It was true for him, and it is true for us today.

Believe it!

INTERLUDE

The Hebrew word translated "daysman" in Job 9:33 means "to act as umpire." The "daysman" is the one with authority to set the day when competing parties come together to settle their dispute. In the East, the "daysman" put his hands on the heads of the two disputing parties to remind them that he was the one with the authority to settle the question. Job longed for somebody who could do this for him and God.

Job was serious about wanting to face God in court, even though he had nobody to represent him. "I desire to reason [argue my case] with God" (13:3). "I will defend mine own ways before Him" (v. 15). "Behold now, I have ordered my cause [prepared my case]; I know that I shall be justified" (v. 18). He felt that God was not treating him justly. "I cry aloud, but there is no justice" (19:7). God had "taken away" his "right" (27:2), and Job demanded an opportunity to be heard before the throne of God. But when the opportunity came, Job had nothing to say.

"It is not why I suffer that I wish to know, but only whether I suffer for Your sake."

Levi Yitzhak of Berditcher

An Angry "Younger" Man

Job's three friends were old men, so Zophar must have been the youngest since he spoke last. His first speech is not long; but what it lacks in length, it makes up for in animosity, for it reveals that Zophar was angry. There is a proper time and place for the display of righteous anger (Eph. 4:26), but Job's ash heap was not the place, and that was not the right time. "The wrath of man does not produce the righteousness of God" (James 1:20, NKJV). What Job needed was a helping hand, not a slap in the face.

Zophar makes three accusations against Job: Job is guilty of sin (Job 11:1-4); Job is ignorant of God (vv. 5-12); and Job is stubborn in his refusal to repent (vv. 13-20). In his reply, Job answers all three accusations: He affirms God's greatness (Job 12) and his own innocence (Job 13), but he has no hope, so why should he repent? (Job 14)

1. Zophar's three accusations (Job 11:1-20)
After listening to Eliphaz and Bildad accuse Job, Zophar should have had enough sense and compassion to take a new approach. Job would hold fast to his integrity no matter what God did or his friends said, so why continue that discussion?

45

How sad it is when people who should share ministry end up creating misery. "Rejoice with them that do rejoice, and weep with them that weep" (Rom. 12:15) is good counsel to follow.

"Job is guilty!" (Job 11:1-4) Like Bildad (8:2), Zophar opened his address by calling Job a "windbag." How tragic that these three friends focused on Job's words instead of the feelings behind those words. A Chinese proverb says, "Though conversing face to face, their hearts have a thousand miles between them." How true that was at the ash heap! After all, information is not the same as communication. Sidney J. Harris reminds us, "Information is giving out; communication is getting through."

Not only was Job's speech a lot of wind, but it was also chatter ("lies") and mockery (11:3). What Job said about God was not true and could only be compared to the idle chatter of people who speak without thinking. And what Job said about himself was an outright lie, for he was not pure before God. In maintaining his integrity, Job gave the impression that he was sinless, which, of course, was not true. (See 6:30; 9:20-21; 10:7.)

Job is ignorant of God (Job 11:5-12). Zophar's request in verse 5 was answered when God appeared (38:1); but it was Zophar and his two friends who were later rebuked by God, and not Job! Job was commended by the Lord for telling the truth. Beware of asking God to tell others what they need to know, unless you are willing for Him to show *you* what you need to know.

Zophar wanted Job to grasp the height, depth, breadth, and length of God's divine wisdom (11:8-9). In saying this, Zophar was hinting that he himself already knew the vast dimensions of God's wisdom and could teach Job if he would listen. It's too bad Zophar didn't know the vast dimensions of God's love (Eph. 3:17-19) and share some of that love with Job.

46

When Zophar said that the secrets of God's wisdom were "double" (Job 11:6), what did he mean? It could mean that God's wisdom is full and complete (Isa. 40:2), or that God has twice as much wisdom as Job thinks He has. The NIV says that "true wisdom has two sides" (Job 11:6). There is the small side that we see and the huge side that only God can see.

Since God knows everything, He knows all about Job and could punish him more than He has. "It could be worse!" is certainly no comfort to a man who has lost his family, his wealth, and his health, and is barely hanging on to life. You don't measure suffering in a quantitative way the way you measure produce at the supermarket. The flippant way in which Job's friends were speaking about his situation shows they lacked understanding. "The deeper the sorrow," says the Jewish *Talmud*, "the less tongue it has."

The two questions in verse 7 expect a negative answer. Nobody can "fathom the mysteries of God" or "probe the limits of the Almighty" (NIV). Of course, Job never claimed to know everything about God; but what he did know encouraged him to hold fast to his integrity and not give up.

God is not accountable to us. He can arrest and imprison anybody He chooses, convene the court and pronounce the sentence; and nobody can say a word in protest (v. 10; see 9:12). God knows who is wise and who is foolish, who is pure and who is sinful. Since God has passed judgment on Job, Job must be guilty.

Zophar closed this accusation by quoting a proverb (11:12). It's not easy to ascertain its meaning. The proverb may be saying that no matter how stupid a man is when he is born, even as dumb as a wild donkey, there is still hope for him to become intelligent. Or, the proverb might be saying just the opposite, as in the NIV: "But a witless man can no more become wise than a wild donkey's colt can be born a man."

The NASB agrees: "And an idiot will become intelligent when the foal of a wild donkey is born a man." In view of Zophar's anger and insulting language, it is likely that the NIV and NASB translations are correct.

Job is stubborn and should repent (Job 11:13-20). "There is hope!" is Zophar's encouraging word to Job (v. 18), and he described what Job could experience. God would bless him abundantly, and his troubles would be over. Job could lift up his head again, and his fears would be gone (v. 15; 10:15). He would forget his misery like water gone over the dam (11:16). God would give him a long life, and it would be the dawning of a new day for him (v. 17). He would dwell in the light, not in the darkness of Sheol (10:20-22); and God's security would put an end to all his fears (11:19-20).

But if Job wanted these blessings, he had to get them on Zophar's terms. Yes, there was hope, but it was hope with a condition attached to it: Job must repent and confess his sins (vv. 13-14). *Zophar is tempting Job to bargain with God so he can get out of his troubles.* This is exactly what Satan wanted Job to do! "Doth Job fear God for nothing?" Satan asked (1:9). Satan accused Job of having a "commercial faith" that promised prosperity in return for obedience. If Job had followed Zophar's advice, he would have played right into the hands of the enemy.

Job did not have a "commercial faith" that made bargains with God. He had a confident faith that said, "Though He slay me, yet will I trust in Him" (13:15). That doesn't sound like a man looking for an easy way out of difficulties. "Job did not understand the Lord's reasons," said C.H. Spurgeon, "but he continued to confide in His goodness." That is faith!

2. Job's three affirmations (Job 12–14)

Zophar's speech was a brief one, but Job took a long time to answer each of Zophar's accusations. Job began with Zophar's second accusation that Job had no knowledge of God (Job 11:5-12). Job affirmed that he had wisdom and understanding just as they did (Job 12). Then he replied to Zophar's first accusation that Job was a guilty sinner (11:1-4). Job once again affirmed his integrity (Job 13). Job then closed his speech by challenging Zophar's third point, that there was still hope (11:13-20). In Job 14, Job admits that his hope is almost gone.

The greatness of God (Job 12). First, Job challenged his friends' declaration that they had more wisdom than he did. True, they were older than Job; but age is no guarantee of wisdom. There are old fools as well as young fools.

Then, Job rebuked them for being so unfeeling toward him and turning him into a laughingstock. He felt he was just and upright, which is the way God described him (1:1, 8; 2:3). "You who are at ease have no concern for people who are slipping. You say God is punishing me for my sins. Then why doesn't He punish robbers and other people who provoke God?" (12:5-6) Zophar claimed that wisdom was not accessible to man (11:7-9), but Job said that God's creatures could teach them what they needed to know (12:7-11; see Gen. 1:26-28). Even "dumb" creatures know that God's hand made everything and keeps everything going. In fact, the very breath they were using to accuse Job was God's gift to them; and He could remove it without their permission. God gave men and women the ability to taste and judge food. Would He not give them the even more important ability to evaluate words and assess truth? (Job 12:11)

In verses 12-25, Job describes the wisdom and power of God. Verse 12 likely refers to God, "the Ancient One" and "the One who lives long." These divine names are a rebuke to Job's aged friends who thought that their years of experience had taught them so much!

Job pointed out that God is completely sovereign in what

He does with nature (vv. 14-15) and with people (vv. 16-25). What He destroys cannot be rebuilt, and what He locks up cannot be released (Rev. 3:6-8). He can send drought or flood, and nobody can stop Him (Job 12:15). He has the wisdom to know what to do, and He has the power to accomplish it (vv. 13, 16).

In His sovereignty over people, no matter what their status, God is in control. Job's argument is that all kinds of people experience difficulties in life because God can do what He pleases. He is no respecter of persons and is not impressed by a person's rank, wealth, or social status.

For example, if it is God's will, king's counselors will lose their authority and wealth, and judges will become confused and mad. In fact, kings themselves will lose their girdles (an insignia of authority), and priests ("princes," v. 19, KJV) will be stripped and become captives. Wise people like counselors and elders will be silenced (v. 20), and princes (nobles) and the mighty (v. 21) will lose their respect and strength.

But God is sovereign over nations as well as individuals (vv. 23-25; Dan. 2:20-22; Acts 17:24-28). He can enlarge a nation or destroy it, or give it freedom or bondage. All He has to do is take wisdom away from the leaders, and the nation's destruction is sure. Proud people don't like to hear this message. Ever since the city of Enoch (Gen. 4:16-18) and the Tower of Babel (11:1-9), mankind has been trying to build and manage things without God; and the end has always been failure and judgment.

The integrity of Job (Job 13). In this part of his defense, Job first expressed his *disappointment* in his three friends (vv. 1-12), then his *declaration* of faith in the Lord (vv. 13-17), and finally his *desire* that God come to him and get the issue settled once and for all (vv. 18-28).

(1) Disappointment (vv. 1-12). Job's friends had not been an encouragement to him. They had taken a superior attitude as

judges, assuming that they knew God better than Job did. They did not identify with him in his grief and pain. Job called them "forgers of lies," "physicians of no value," and "deceitful defenders of God."

The word "forgers" (v. 4) also means "whitewashers." They smeared the whitewash of their lies over the discussion so that they avoided the difficult problems while maintaining their traditional ideas (Ps. 119:69). They stayed on the surface of things and never went deep into God's truth or Job's feelings. Counseling that stays on the surface will accomplish very little. If we are going to help people, we must go much deeper; but this demands love, courage, and patience.

As physicians, their diagnosis was wrong so their remedy was useless (Jer. 6:14; 8:11). And as "defenders of God," they would be better off silent; for they did not know what they were talking about. They had such a rigid and narrow view of God, and such a prejudiced view of Job, that their whole "case" was a fabrication of lies. What would they do when God turned the tables and examined them? (See Rom. 14:1-13.) "Your maxims are proverbs of ashes; your defenses are defenses of clay" (Job 13:12, NIV). What the three friends thought were profound statements of truth were only warmed-over ashes from ancient fires, clay pots that would fall apart. A good counselor needs much more than a good memory. He or she also needs wisdom to know how to apply the truth to the needs of people today.

(2) Declaration (vv. 13-17). This is one of the greatest declarations of faith found anywhere in Scripture, but it must be understood in its context. Job is saying, "I will take my case directly to God and prove my integrity. I know I am taking my life in my hands in approaching God, because He is able to slay me. But if He doesn't slay me, it is proof that I am not the hypocrite you say I am." Later, Job will take an oath and challenge God to pass judgment (Job 27). To approach God

personally was a great act of faith (Ex. 33:20; Jud. 13:22-23), but Job was so sure of his integrity that he would take his chances. After all, if he did nothing, he would die; and if he was rejected by God, he would die; but there was always the possibility that God would prove him right.

(3) Desire (vv. 18-28). These words are addressed to God. Job has "prepared his case" (v. 18, NIV) and is sure that he will win. Job has two desires: that God would remove His chastening hand and give Job relief, and that God would come to Job in such a way that He would not frighten him. Job is asking God to meet him in court so they can talk over God's "case" against Job and Job's "case" against God. In verse 22, Job gives God the option of speaking first!

Why does Job want to meet God in court? So that God can once and for all state His "case" against Job and let Job know the sins in his life that have caused him to suffer so much. "Why should God pay so much attention to me?" asks Job. "He treats me like an enemy, but I'm just a weak leaf in the wind, a piece of chaff that is worth nothing. I'm a piece of rotting wood and a moth-eaten garment, yet God treats me like a prisoner of war and watches me every minute." Job felt the time had come to settle the matter, even if it meant losing his own life in the process.

The hopelessness of Job (Job 14). Zophar had assured Job that there was hope for him if only he would acknowledge his sins and repent (Job 11:13-20). But Zophar was not in Job's situation! From Job's point of view, his future was bleak. In verses 1-12, Job used several images to illustrate the hopeless condition of man in this world. He is like a flower that is soon cut down, a shadow that slowly disappears, a hired man that puts in his time and then is replaced. God knows the limits of our days (7:1; 14:5; Ps. 139:16). A suicide may foolishly hasten the day of death, but nobody will go beyond the limits that God has set for his or her life.

Since man is only a flower, a shadow, and a servant, why should God pay any attention to him? Since life is so short, why should God fill man's few days with grief and pain? "So look away from him and let him alone," prays Job (Job 14:6, NIV). "Let me have some peace before my brief life ends!" (paraphrase)

Job's strongest image is that of the tree (vv. 7-12). Chop it down, and its stump remains, and there is always a possibility that the tree might sprout again. The tree has hope, but man has no hope. When he dies, he leaves no stump behind. Man is more like water that evaporates or soaks into the ground; it can never be recovered again (v. 11; 2 Sam. 14:14). Man may lie down at night and awaken in the morning; but when he lies down in death, there is no assurance that he will be awakened again.

Early believers like Job did not have the revelation of future life as we now have it in Christ (2 Tim. 1:10). Passages in the Old Testament hint at future resurrection (Pss. 16:9-11; 17:15; Isa. 26:19; Dan. 12:2), but Job did not have any of these books to read and ponder. "If a man dies, shall he live again?" (Job 14:14) Job asked this important question but did not answer it. Later on, Job will make a great statement about future resurrection (19:25-26); but at this point he is vacillating between despair and hope.

In 14:13, Job asked God to give Himself a reminder to bring Job back from Sheol, the realm of the dead. Job was probably not thinking of resurrection, but of a brief return to earth so God could vindicate him before his accusers. Of course, a believer today is sealed by the Holy Spirit unto the day of redemption (Eph. 1:13-14); and God will not forget one of His children at the resurrection (1 Cor. 15:50-58).

Job reminded the Lord that he was the work of God's hands (Job 14:15), an argument he had used before (10:3). It seemed to Job that, instead of caring for His creature, God was doing nothing but keeping a record of his sins. What hope could Job have as long as God was investigating him and building a case against him? Instead of cleansing Job's sins, God was covering them and would not even tell Job what they were!

"Thou destroyest the hope of man," Job complained (14:19), and he used two illustrations to make his point. Man seems like a sturdy mountain, but the water gradually erodes the rock, and it eventually crumbles. Or an earthquake might suddenly move the rocks from one place to another and change the mountain. Death may come gradually or suddenly, but it will come; and man will go to a world where he knows nothing about what his family is doing. Job longed for that release from sorrow and pain.

When people are experiencing intense grief and pain, it is easy for them to feel that the future is hopeless and that God has forsaken them. The eminent American psychiatrist Karl Menninger called hope "the major weapon against the suicide impulse." Hopeless people feel that life is not worth living since they have nothing to look forward to but suffering and failure. They conclude that it is better for them to die than to live and be a burden to themselves and to others.

The German philosopher Friedrich Nietzsche called hope "the worst of all evils, because it prolongs the torments of man." But an individual who believes in Jesus Christ shares in a "living hope" that grows more wonderful every day (1 Peter 1:3ff). Dead hopes fade away because they have no roots, but our "living hope" gets better because it is rooted in the living Christ and His Living Word. The assurance of resurrection and life in glory with Christ is a strong motivation for us to keep going even when the going is tough (1 Cor. 15:58).

Charles L. Allen has written, "When you say a situation or a person is hopeless, you are slamming the door in the face of

God." Job had not yet slammed the door, but he was getting close to doing it; and his friends were not helping him at all.

"Now may the God of hope fill you with all joy and peace in believing, that you may abound in hope by the power of the Holy Spirit" (Rom. 15:13, NASB).

"How rarely we weigh our neighbor in the same balance in which we weigh ourselves."

Thomas à Kempis

Discussion Turns into Dispute

During this second round of speeches, the fire becomes hotter as the three friends focus more on proving Job wrong than on giving Job help. After all, their own peace of mind was at stake; and they were not about to surrender. If Job was not a sinner being punished by God, then the three friends' understanding of God was all wrong. *But that meant they had no protection against personal suffering themselves!* If obedience is not a guarantee of health and wealth, then what happened to Job might happen to them. God forbid!

An anonymous wit once described a theologian as "a blind man in a dark room searching for a black cat that isn't there—and finding it!" But a true theologian walks in the light of God's revelation in His Word, in history, and in creation; and he humbly accepts the truth, no matter what the cost.

Job's three friends were not true theologians because they saw only one side of the picture, the side they wanted to see. The longshoreman-philosopher, Eric Hoffer, wrote, "We are least open to precise knowledge concerning the things we are most vehement about." And also the things we are most fearful about!

1. Eliphaz: two warnings (Job 15)

In his first speech (Job 4–5), Eliphaz had displayed some kindness toward Job; but you find neither patience nor kindness in this second address. Nor do you find any new ideas: Eliphaz merely repeats his former thesis that man is a sinner and God must punish sinners (5:17-19). He issued two warnings to Job.

Job lacks wisdom (Job 15:1-16). How did Eliphaz know this? For one thing, he had listened to *Job's words* (vv. 1-6) and found them to be nothing but wind. Job's ideas were only "empty notions" and "useless words" (vv. 2-3, NIV). Job's words came from a belly filled with the hot desert wind (Jonah 4:8) and not from a heart filled with true wisdom. Eliphaz was using one of the oldest tactics in debate—if you can't refute your opponent's arguments, attack his words and make them sound like a lot of "hot air."

Samuel Johnson was the "literary czar" of eighteenth-century England, a man who loved to sit by the hour with his friends and discuss any and all topics. But Johnson always had to win the argument, whether he was right or not. The poet and playwright Oliver Goldsmith said, "There is no arguing with Johnson; for if his pistol misses fire, he knocks you down with the butt end of it!" Eliphaz was like that.

Eliphaz not only heard Job's words, but he *saw where those words led* (Job 15:4). "But you even undermine piety and hinder devotion to God" (v. 4, NIV). If everybody believed as Job believed—that God does not always punish the wicked and reward the godly—then what motive would people have for obeying God? Religion would not be worth it! *But this is the devil's theology, the very thing that God was using Job to refute!* If people serve God only for what they get out of it, then they are not serving God at all, they are only serving themselves by making God their servant. Their "religion" is only a pious system for promoting selfishness and not for glorifying God.

When God called Israel and established His covenant with her, the people's motive for obedience was fear of punishment. If they obeyed the law, God would bless them; if they disobeyed, He would punish them. But this was during the infancy of the nation, when God dealt with them as with children. Children understand rewards and punishments far better than they do ethics and morality. But when the new generation was about to enter Canaan, Moses gave them a higher motive for obedience: their love for God (Deut. 6:4-5; 7:7; 10:12-16; 11:1, 13, 22; 19:9). They were no longer children, and God didn't need to frighten them (or "bribe" them) into obeying Him. Love is the fulfillment of the law (Rom. 13:8-10) and the highest motive for obedience (John 14:15).

Job's words told Eliphaz that Job had a *wicked heart* (Job 15:5-6). "Your sins are telling your mouth what to say!" (v. 5, TLB; see Matt. 12:34-37) Job was affirming his innocence, but Eliphaz interpreted his words as proving Job's guilt! What hope was there for Job when his friends would not even believe what he was saying?

Job lacked wisdom because *he lacked experience* (Job 15:7-10). At this point, Eliphaz turned on the sarcasm, another proof that he has run out of something intelligent to say. This is another debater's trick: when you can't refute the speech, ridicule the speaker. Job never claimed that he was the first man God created, that he was God's confidant, or that God had given him a monopoly on wisdom. Job knew that his friends were older than he was, but age is no guarantee of wisdom (32:9; Ps. 119:97-104).

According to Eliphaz, Job's attitude was wrong because he refused God's help (Job 15:11-16). Eliphaz saw himself and his friends as God's messengers, sent to bring Job the consolation he needed. Their words were "spoken gently" (v. 11, NIV), but Job's words were spoken in anger. The three friends were serving God, but Job was resisting God.

Then Eliphaz repeated the message he had given in his first speech (vv. 14-16; 4:17-19). Job had refused to accept it the first time, but perhaps he would accept it now that he had suffered more. If heaven is not pure before God, nor the angels that inhabit heaven, how can a mere man claim to be innocent? Man is born with a sinful nature and has a thirst for sin, and Job was no exception. All of this prepared the way for Eliphaz's second warning.

God judges the wicked (Job 15:17-35). In his first speech, Eliphaz had described the blessings of the godly man (5:17-26); but now he describes the sufferings of the ungodly man. Eliphaz was careful to remind Job that these were not his ideas alone, but that the ancients all agreed with him. If Job rejected what Eliphaz said, he was turning his back on the wisdom of their fathers. Eliphaz was a man who found great strength in tradition, forgetting that "tradition is a guide and not a jailer" (W. Somerset Maugham).

When you read this description of a wicked man, you realize that Eliphaz is talking about Job. Job was in pain, darkness, trouble, anguish, and fear. He was defying God and challenging God to meet him and prove him guilty. The fire had destroyed Job's sheep (1:16; 15:30, 34); invaders had stolen his camels (1:17; 15:21); he had lost all his wealth (v. 29); and his eldest son's house had been destroyed by wind and all Job's children with it (1:19; 15:28). Eliphaz was not at all subtle in his approach; everybody knew he was talking about Job.

But in his closing words (vv. 34-35), Eliphaz gave the hardest blow of all: He called Job a hypocrite and a godless man, and he blamed him for the tragedies that had befallen him and his family. Job had secretly "conceived" sin, and now sin had given birth to suffering and death (James 1:14-15; Isa. 59:4; Ps. 7:14). "Their womb fashions deceit" is the NIV rendering of Job 15:35, and the word translated "womb" is the same as "belly" in verse 1. According to Eliphaz, if you x-rayed Job, all you would find would be hot air and sin! "Hypocrite" is a key word in the vocabulary of Job's three friends. Bildad suggested that Job was a hypocrite (8:13), and both Zophar and Elihu will take up the theme (20:5; 34:30; 36:13). Of course, Job denied the accusation (13:16; 17:8; 27:8) and argued that neither God nor his friends could prove it true.

The problem with Eliphaz's statement about the judgment of the wicked is that *it is not always true in this life.* Many wicked people go through life apparently happy and successful, while many godly people experience suffering and seeming failure. It is true that *ultimately* the wicked suffer and the godly are blessed; but, meanwhile, it often looks like the situation is reversed (Ps. 73; Jer. 12:1-4). Furthermore, God gives sunshine to the evil and the good and sends rain on the just and the unjust (Matt. 5:45). He is long-suffering toward sinners (2 Peter 3:9) and waits for His goodness to lead them to repentance (Rom. 2:4; Luke 15:17-19).

The greatest judgment God could send to the wicked in this life would be to *let them have their own way.* "They have their reward" (Matt. 6:2, 5, 16). The only heaven the godless will know is the enjoyment they have on earth in this life, and God is willing for them to have it. The only suffering the godly will experience is in this life, for in heaven there will be no pain or tears. Furthermore, the suffering that God's people experience now is working *for* them and will one day lead to glory (1 Peter 1:6-8; 5:10; 2 Cor. 4:16-18; Rom. 8:18). Eliphaz and his friends had the situation all confused.

2. Job: three requests (Job 16–17)
Job's response is to utter three heartfelt requests: first, a plea to his friends for sympathy (Job 16:1-14); then, a plea to God for justice (vv. 15-22); and finally, a plea to God to end his life and relieve him of suffering (17:1-16).

A plea for sympathy (Job 16:1-14). Job's friends still had not identified with his situation; they did not feel his agony or understand his perplexity. Job had already called them deceitful brooks (see 6:15) and "worthless physicians" (13:4, NIV), but now he calls them "miserable comforters" (16:2). All of their attempts to comfort him only made him more miserable! As the saying goes, "With friends like you, who needs enemies?"

Job assured them that, if they were in his shoes, he would treat them with more understanding than they were showing him. Instead of making long speeches, he would give them words of encouragement. He would listen with his heart and try to help them bear their burdens. Sometimes we have to experience misunderstanding from unsympathetic friends in order to learn how to minister to others. This was a new experience for Job, and he was trying to make the most of it. However, whether Job spoke or kept quiet, he was still a suffering man (v. 6).

In his appeal for loving sympathy, Job told his friends what he was receiving from the hand of God (vv. 7-14). Job is worn out; his family is gone; he is gaunt and weak. Both men and God attack him. Job feels like God has painted a target on his back and handed everybody bows and arrows! There is no relief—God keeps assaulting him like a relentless warrior. "I didn't attack God—He attacked me!" God was his enemy (16:9; 13:24), and nothing Job could do would bring about a truce. If Job looked up, God was against him. If he looked around, his friends were against him. Where could he turn?

A plea for justice (Job 16:15-22). How had Job responded to God's attacks? He put on sackcloth, wept in humiliation and contrition, and buried his face in the dust. In spite of the accusations of Eliphaz (15:4-6), Job knew he was right before God and that God would hear his prayers (16:17).

Job was caught on the horns of a dilemma. His suffering

was so great that he longed to die, but he didn't want to die before he could vindicate himself or see God vindicate him. This explains his cry in verse 18: "O earth, do not cover my blood, and let my cry have no resting place!" (NKJV) The ancients believed that the blood of innocent victims cried out to God for justice (Gen. 4:8-15) and that the spirits of the dead were restless until the corpses were properly buried (Isa. 26:21). Even if Job died, he would be restless until he had been proved righteous by the Lord.

Job's repeated cry has been for a fair trial before the Lord (Job 9:1-4, 14-16, 19-20, 28-35; 10:2; 13:6-8, 19). He has lamented the fact that he had no advocate to represent him before God's throne (9:33). None of his friends would defend him, so his only hope was that God in heaven would defend him and bear witness to his integrity (16:19). But Job yearned for someone to plead with God on his behalf (v. 21).

The Christian believer has this heavenly Advocate in Jesus Christ (1 John 2:1-2). As our interceding High Priest, Christ gives us the conquering grace we need when we are tempted and tested (Heb. 2:17-18; 4:14-16). If we fail, then He is our Advocate to forgive us and restore us when we confess our sins to Him (1 John 1:5–2:2).

Of course, Job wanted a "lawyer" to plead his case before God and convince Him that he was innocent. Once Job had won his case, then God would vindicate him before his critical friends and restore Job's honor. God's people don't need that kind of intercession because the Father and the Son are in perfect agreement in their love for us and their plan for our lives. The Lord Jesus ever lives to make intercession for His people (Rom. 8:31-39; Heb. 7:25) and to perfect them in the will of God (13:20-21). We come to a throne of grace, not a throne of judgment; and we have confidence that our loving Father will do that which is best for us.

A plea for death (Job 17:1-16). One reason Job wanted his

heavenly Advocate to act quickly was because he sensed that death was very near, "the journey of no return" (Job 16:22, NIV). When people suffer so much that their "spirit is broken" (17:1, NIV, NASB), then they lose their "fight" and want life to end.

Job's friends were against him and would not go to court and "post bond" for him (vv. 3-5). People treated Job as if he were the scum of the earth (v. 6). His body was only the shadow of what it had been (v. 7), and all of his plans had been shattered (v. 11). His friends would not change their minds and come to his defense (v. 10). In fact, they would not face his situation honestly, but they kept telling him that the light would soon dawn for him (v. 12). Is it any wonder that Job saw in death the only way of escape?

However, at no time did Job ever consider taking his own life or asking someone else to do it for him. Life is a sacred gift from God, and only God can give it and take it away. On the one hand, Job wanted to live long enough to see himself vindicated; but on the other hand, he didn't know how much more he could endure. Once he was in Sheol, the realm of the dead, he could not be vindicated on earth unless God brought him back.

Job pictured Sheol as his home, where he would lie down in the darkness and be at rest (v. 13). Since he had no family, he would adopt the pit (or "corruption") as his father and the devouring worm as his mother or sister. They would give him more comfort than his friends!

But would there be any hope in the grave? Could Job take his hope with him to Sheol? Paul answers the question: "If in this life only we have hope in Christ, we are of all men the most pitiable. But now Christ is risen from the dead, and has become the firstfruits of those who have fallen asleep" (1 Cor. 15:19-20, NKJV). *Our hope does not die, nor is it buried and left to decay; for our hope is a "living hope" because Christ has won the victory over death and the grave!* Christians sorrow, but they must not sorrow "as others who have no hope" (1 Thes. 4:13).

God did not answer Job's plea for death because He had something far better planned for him. God looked beyond Job's depression and bitterness and saw that he still had faith. When I was a young pastor, I heard an experienced saint say, "I have lived long enough to be thankful for unanswered prayer." At the time, I was shocked by the statement; but now that I have lived a few more years myself, I know what she was talking about. In the darkness of despair and the prison of pain, we often say things that we later regret; *but God understands all about it and lovingly turns a deaf ear to our words but a tender eye to our wounds.*

If only the next speaker would have expressed compassion to this hurting man! But Bildad is all primed to frighten Job out of his wits with the most vivid pictures of death found anywhere in Scripture.

INTERLUDE

The best way to help discouraged and hurting people is to listen with your heart and not just with your ears. It's not what they say but *why they say it* that is important. Let them know that you understand their pain by reflecting back to them *in different words* just what they say to you. Don't argue or try to convince them with logical reasoning. There will be time for that later; meanwhile, patiently accept their feelings—even their bitter words against God—and build bridges, not walls.

In his book about his wife's death, *A Grief Observed*, C.S. Lewis wrote from his own painful experience: "Talk to me about the truth of religion, and I'll listen gladly. Talk to me about the duty of religion, and I'll listen submissively. But don't come talking to me about the consolation of religion, or I shall suspect you don't understand" (p. 23).

There is true consolation in our faith, but it is not dispensed in convenient doses like cough medicine. *It can be shared only by those who know what it's like to be so far down in the pit that they feel as though God has abandoned them.* If you want to be a true comforter, there is a price to pay; and not everybody is willing to pay it. Paul wrote about this in 2 Corinthians 1:3-11.

John Henry Jowett said, "God does not comfort us to make us comfortable, but to make us comforters." God's comfort is never *given;* it is always *loaned.* God expects us to share it with others.

"Death is the great adventure, beside which moon landings and space trips pale into insignificance."

Joseph Bayly

Will the Real Enemy Please Stand Up?

Bildad opened his second speech with the same words he used in his first speech: "How long?" (Job 18:2; 8:2) and Job said the same thing when he replied (19:2). The friends were growing impatient with each other because their conversation seemed to be getting nowhere. George Bernard Shaw compared the average conversation to "a phonograph with half-a-dozen records—you soon get tired of them all."

Bildad blamed Job for the stalemate and admonished him, "Be sensible, and then we can talk" (18:2, NIV). It never dawned on Bildad that he and his two friends were playing the same tunes over and over again: (1) God is just; (2) God punishes the wicked and blesses the righteous; (3) since Job is suffering, he must be wicked; (4) if he turns from his sins, God will again bless him. They were going around in circles.

Bildad said that Job was not being sensible, nor was he being respectful. He was treating his friends like dumb cattle instead of like the wise men they really were (v. 3). Job was also being irritable and displaying anger instead of humility (v. 4). "Is God supposed to rearrange the whole world just for you?" Bildad asks. "Should He ravage the land with war or even send an earthquake just because of you?" Eliphaz wasn't the only one who knew how to use sarcasm!

However, Bildad planned to use a stronger weapon than sarcasm. His weapon was *fear*. If the three friends could not reason with Job, or shame Job into repenting, perhaps they could frighten Job by describing what happens when wicked people die.

Before we study Bildad's terrifying speech, we should note that fear is a normal human emotion and there is nothing wrong with it. We use the fear of sickness, injury, or death to teach children to wash their hands, stay away from power lines, and look carefully before crossing the street. Fear of financial loss motivates people to buy insurance, and fear of death encourages them to have an annual physical checkup.

Fear of death (and the judgment that follows) is a legitimate motive for trusting Jesus Christ and being saved. "And do not fear those who kill the body but cannot kill the soul," said Jesus. "But rather fear Him who is able to destroy both soul and body in hell" (Matt. 10:28, NKJV). Jesus preached a gracious message of love, but He also preached a stern message of judgment. Paul wrote, "Knowing, therefore, the terror of the Lord, we persuade men" (2 Cor. 5:11). When Jonathan Edwards preached his sermon "Sinners in the Hands of an Angry God," he did not violate any psychological or biblical principles. The emotions of nonbelievers must be stirred before their minds can be instructed and their wills challenged.

However, Bildad made two mistakes when he gave this speech about the horrors of death. To begin with, he preached it to the wrong man; for Job was already a believer (Job 1:1, 8). Second, he preached it with the wrong motive, for there was no love in his heart. Dr. R.W. Dale, the British preacher, once asked evangelist D.L. Moody if he ever used "the element of terror" in his preaching. Moody replied that he usually preached one sermon on heaven and one on hell in each of his campaigns, but that a "man's heart ought to be very tender" when preaching about the doom of the lost. Bildad did not have a tender heart.

1. The terrors of death (Job 18:5-21)

In this address, Bildad painted four vivid pictures of the death of the wicked.

A light put out (Job 18:5-6). Light is associated with life just as darkness is associated with death. Since God is the author of life, He alone can "light our lamp"; for "He gives to all life, breath, and all things," and "in Him we live and move and have our being" (Acts 17:25, 28, NKJV). The picture here is that of a lamp hanging in a tent and a fire smoldering in a fire pot. Suddenly, the lamp goes out, and the last spark of the fire vanishes, and the tent is in total darkness (Prov. 13:9; 24:20).

Like the flame of the lamp or the spark in the coals, life is a precious but delicate thing. It doesn't take a very strong wind to blow it out. "There is but a step between me and death" (1 Sam. 20:3). The American newspaper magnate William Randolph Hearst would never permit anybody to mention death in his presence. Yet on August 14, 1951, the flame of his life went out, and he died. "The spirit of man is the lamp of the Lord" (Prov. 20:27), and God can blow out that lamp whenever He pleases.

A traveler trapped (Job 18:7-10). Frightened, the man leaves his tent and starts down the road, looking for a place of safety. But the road turns out to be the most dangerous place of all, for it is punctuated by traps. Bildad used six different words to describe the dangers people face when they try to run away from death:

> *a net*—spread across the path to catch him
> *a snare*—branches covering a deep pit

68

    a trap—a "gin" (snare) with a noose that springs when
touched; he is caught by the heel
    a robber—another pitfall
    a snare—a noose hidden on the ground
    a trap—any device that catches prey

These devices were used to catch birds and animals, not
people; but the wicked person is like a beast because he has
left God out of his life.

No matter what schemes the traveler invents, he cannot
escape the traps; and the more he tries, the weaker he becomes (Job 18:7). Darkness and danger surround him, and
there is no hope.

A criminal pursued (Job 18:11-15). Death is "the king of
terrors" (v. 14), determined to arrest the culprit no matter
where he is. If the escaped criminal runs on the path and
escapes the traps, then death will send some of his helpers to
chase him. Terror frightens him, calamity eats away at his
strength, and disaster waits for him to fall (vv. 11-12, NIV).

The frightened criminal gets weaker and weaker but still
tries to keep going. If he goes back to his tent to hide, the
pursuers find him, arrest him, drag him out, and take him to
the king of terrors. They take everything out of his tent, burn
the tent, and then scatter sulfur over the ashes. The end of
that man is fire and brimstone!

A tree rooted up (Job 18:16-21). Sometimes death is not as
dramatic and sudden as the arresting of a criminal. Death may
be gradual, like the dying of a tree. The roots dry up, the
branches start to wither, and the dead branches are cut off
one by one. Soon the tree is completely dead, and men chop
it down. The death of a tree illustrates the extinction of a
family, a "family tree." Not only is the wicked man himself
cut down, but all the branches are cut down too; and he
leaves no descendants to carry on his name. (Remember, all

of Job's children had been killed by the great wind.) In the East, the extinction of a family was viewed as a great tragedy.

Job had used a tree as an illustration of the hope of resurrection (14:7-11), but Bildad did not agree with him. According to Bildad, once the tree is down, that is the end; the wicked man has no future hope.

Though Bildad was talking to the wrong man and with the wrong motive, what he said about death should be taken seriously. Death is an enemy to be feared by all who are not prepared to die (1 Cor. 15:26), and the only way to be prepared is to trust Jesus Christ (John 5:24).

For the Christian believer, death means going home to the Father in heaven (John 14:1-6), falling asleep on earth and waking up in heaven (Acts 7:60; Phil. 1:21-23), entering into rest (Rev. 14:13), and moving into greater light (Prov. 4:18). None of the pictures Bildad used should be applied to those who have trusted the Lord for salvation.

2. The trials of life (Job 19:1-29)

When Bildad finished describing the terrors of death, Job replied by describing the trials of life, *his own life*. "I don't have to *die* to experience trials," he said to his friends. "I'm experiencing them right now, and you don't seem to care!"

Insults (Job 19:1-4). Our words either hurt others or heal them; we either add to their burdens or help them bear their burdens with courage. Job's friends crushed him with their words; they made him feel worthless and helpless in the face of all his suffering. How sensitive we should be to the needs and struggles of others! Even if people do need rebuke, we should do it in love; and our words should hearten them and not weaken them.

"Even if I have sinned," Job said in 19:4, "it's *my* sin and not yours. God and I can work things out, so leave me alone." The word Job used ("erred") means "an unintentional sin."

Job still defended his integrity and claimed that he had committed no sins worthy of all the suffering he had endured.

Illustrations (Job 19:5-12). Bildad had given four frightening pictures of the terrors of death, so Job countered with seven vivid pictures of the trials of his life, what he was experiencing right then and there!

He felt like *an animal trapped* (v. 6). Job saw himself caught in God's net, not because of his sins but because God had trapped him. Bildad described six different kinds of traps that would catch a fleeing criminal (18:7-10), but Job did not put himself into that picture. He was not running away from God, nor was he guilty of sin. It was God who had suddenly caught him for reasons Job did not understand.

He also felt like *a criminal in court* (19:7). God had wronged him by arresting him and bringing him into judgment. What had he done? Why were the charges not read to him? Why was he not permitted a defense? "Though I call for help, there is no justice" (v. 7, NIV). Throughout the book, Job pleads for justice and cries out for an advocate to defend himself before God. What Job did not realize was that *he was the advocate defending God!* It was Job's faith and endurance that proved Satan wrong and brought glory to the Lord.

Job saw himself as *a traveler fenced in* (v. 8). Satan had complained that God had "walled in" Job and his family so that they were protected from trouble (1:9-12). Now Job is complaining because God has blocked his path, and he cannot move. Job could not see what lay ahead because God had shrouded the way with darkness.

At times God permits His children to experience darkness on a dead-end street where they don't know which way to turn. When this happens, *wait for the Lord to give you light in His own time.* Don't try to manufacture your own light or to borrow light from others. Follow the wise counsel of Isaiah, "Who among you fears the Lord? Who obeys the voice of His

Servant? Who walks in darkness and has no light? Let him trust in the name of the Lord and rely upon his God" (Isa. 50:10, NKJV).

Dr. Bob Jones, Sr. used to say, "Never doubt in the darkness what God has taught you in the light." In fact, what God teaches us in the light will become even more meaningful in the darkness.

"Oh, the unspeakable benediction of the 'treasures of darkness'!" wrote Oswald Chambers. "It is not the days of sunshine and splendor and liberty and light that leave their lasting and indelible effect upon the soul, but those nights of the Spirit in which, shadowed by God's hand, hidden in the dark cleft of some rock in a weary land, He lets the splendors of the outskirts of Himself pass before our gaze."

Job's suffering left him feeling like *a king dethroned* (Job 19:9). Before his calamities came, Job had been the leading man in Uz and the greatest man in the East (1:3; 29:1-25); but now all that honor and authority were gone. God had taken from him his royal robes and crown, and now he was the lowest instead of the highest. What humiliation!

His fifth picture is that of *a structure destroyed* (19:10). It could be a wall or a building that God's "troops" swooped down on and left in ruins. Job may have been looking back at his business affairs or his household; or perhaps he was contemplating his emaciated body. In any event, what was once strong and useful was now useless and destroyed. Bildad had spoken about a tent being destroyed (18:15), and Job knew what this meant.

In the sixth picture, Job borrowed the image of *a tree uprooted* (19:10; see 18:16). Job had used the tree as a picture of hope (14:7), but now he sees it as a symbol of *lost* hope. But in Job 14, Job was speaking about a tree that was chopped down, while here the tree is *uprooted*. Without a root system, the tree cannot live.

Job's final picture is that of *a besieged city* (19:11-12). God has declared war on Job (13:24) and is treating him like an enemy. His troops have attacked him and settled down for a long, hard siege. Imagine a large army building a ramp just to attack a tent! Once again, Job cannot understand why God has sent so much suffering. Why use an atomic bomb just to destroy a tent?

Isolation (Job 19:13-22). Job went on to explain how his suffering affected his relationship with people. We must recognize that extreme and prolonged pain often isolates sufferers from people and circumstances around them. When people really hurt, they may tend to withdraw and give the impression that others don't really understand what they are going through. Job felt alienated from those left in his family, from his friends, and even from his servants.

But there was more to this alienation than Job's pain. He was now bankrupt and ill, living at the city dump; and nobody wanted to be identified with him. Furthermore, people were convinced that Job was a guilty sinner suffering the judgment of God; so why be his friend? His appearance was repulsive, and people avoided looking at him. He was being treated like a leper, an outcast who was not wanted by family or friends.

One evidence of our Lord's compassion was the way He identified with outcasts. He ate with "publicans and sinners" (Matt. 9:9-13), touched the lepers (Matt. 8:1-4), accepted gifts from prostitutes (Luke 7:36-50), and even died between two criminals (23:32-33). Jesus knew what it was like to be "despised and rejected of men, a man of sorrows, and acquainted with grief" (Isa. 53:3). How important it is that we, His disciples, have this same kind of compassion. It's easy to identify with people we know and like when they are going through trials, but we tend to overlook the helpless, the poor, and the neglected in their sufferings.

Job's statement in Job 19:20 has become a familiar but

misunderstood proverb: "I am escaped with the skin of my teeth." This is usually quoted, "I escaped *by* the skin of my teeth," that is, "I just barely escaped!" (If there were skin on our teeth, how thick would it be?) But the Hebrew text says "with" and not "by," and interpreters don't agree on the meaning.

Some suggest that Job meant, "I'm so far gone that only my gums are left!" But the gums are not usually referred to as "the skin of the teeth." Others say that he meant, "If there were skin on my teeth, that's how close I am to death!" Or, "My body is so emaciated that all I have left is the skin of my teeth!" (He was exaggerating, of course.) Whatever Job had in mind, the image clearly shows one thing: it was a miracle that Job was alive.

Job closed this part of his defense by appealing to his friends for pity (vv. 21-22; 6:14). God was against him, his family and friends had deserted him, and all he had left were his three intimate friends who were now pursuing him like wild beasts after their prey. Couldn't they stop and try to help him? Why must they have such hard hearts?

Insight (Job 19:23-29). Why did Job want his words to be recorded permanently? He thought he was going to die before God would vindicate him, and he wanted people to remember how he suffered and what he said. Bildad warned him, "The remembrance of him [a wicked man] shall perish from the earth" (18:17), and Job wanted his record to remain.

At this point, Job uttered another of his statements of faith that in this book punctuate his many expressions of grief and pain. It is significant that Job would go from the depths of despair to the heights of faith, and then back into the depths again. *This is often the normal experience of people experiencing great suffering.* The skies will be dark and stormy, a ray of light will suddenly shine through, and then the storm will come again.

In spite of what some preachers say, very few people can maintain a constant high level of faith and courage in times of severe pain and trial. John Henry Jowett, at one time known as "the greatest preacher in the English-speaking world," wrote to a friend: "I wish you wouldn't think I am such a saint. You seem to imagine that I have no ups and downs, but just a level and lofty stretch of spiritual attainment with unbroken joy and equanimity. By no means! I am often perfectly wretched, and everything appears most murky" (*John Henry Jowett,* by Arthur Porrit, p. 290).

In 19:25-27, Job expressed confidence that, even if he died, he would still have a Redeemer who one day would exercise judgment on the earth. Furthermore, Job affirmed that he himself expected to live again and see his Redeemer! "And after my skin has been destroyed, yet in my flesh I will see God" (v. 26, NIV). It was an affirmation of faith in the resurrection of the human body.

The Hebrew word translated "Redeemer" in verse 25 refers to the kinsman redeemer, the near relative who could avenge his brother's blood (Deut. 19:6-12), reclaim and restore his brother's property (Lev. 25:23-24, 39-55), and set his brother free from slavery (25:25). The kinsman redeemer could also go to court on behalf of a wronged relative (Prov. 23:10-11). In the Book of Ruth, Boaz is the kinsman redeemer who was willing and able to rescue Ruth and give her a new life in a new land.

Previously, Job had talked about his need for an umpire (Job 9:33-34) and an Advocate in heaven (16:19). Now he takes it a step further: his Redeemer will one day vindicate him, and Job will be there to witness it! When you consider how little God had revealed in Job's day about the future life, these words become a remarkable testimony of faith. And when you add to this the discouragement expressed by Job's friends and his own intense suffering, Job's witness becomes even more wonderful.

Of course, this kinsman redeemer is Jesus Christ. He took upon Himself a human nature so that He might reveal God to us, experience all that we experience, die for our sins, and then return to heaven to represent us before the Father. He is *willing* to save and *able* to save. One day He shall stand upon the earth and exercise judgment; and He will vindicate His own people.

Job closed his speech with a word of warning to his three critical friends (19:28-29): They too will stand at God's judgment throne, so they had better be ready. They accused Job of being a sinner, but were *they* not also sinners? They said that God was judging Job for his sins, but will He not judge them as well? One day they will have to answer to God for the way they have spoken to and about Job, so they had better beware. Job's words remind us of Paul's counsel in Romans 14:10-13 and our Lord's warning in Matthew 7:1-5.

Abraham Lincoln once said, "He has a right to criticize who has a heart to help."

Do you qualify?

> *"The truest help we can render an afflicted man is not to take his burden from him, but to call out his best strength that he may be able to bear it."*
>
> **Phillips Brooks**

It All Depends on Your Point of View

Zophar is next in line to speak, but he has nothing new to say. It's the same old story: God punishes the wicked, so Job had better get right with God. His key text is Job 20:5, "The triumphing of the wicked is short, and the joy of the hypocrite but for a moment." This theme has already been discussed by Bildad (8:11-19; 18) and Eliphaz (15:20-35), but Zophar is so disturbed by Job's last speech that he feels he must speak. "I hear a rebuke that dishonors me, and my understanding inspires me to reply" (20:3, NIV). Zophar felt insulted by Job and decided to defend himself.

1. The awful fate of the wicked (Job 20:4-29)

Zophar makes three affirmations to prove that the fate of the wicked is indeed terrible: their life is brief (Job 20:4-11), their pleasure is temporary (vv. 12-19), and their death is painful (vv. 20-29).

Their life is brief (Job 20:4-11). Zophar declares that from the beginning of human history the triumphing ("mirth") of the wicked has been short. We wonder where he got his information, for the Lord waited 120 years before sending the Flood (Gen. 6:3), and God gave the wicked Canaanites at least four centuries before He judged them (15:13-16).

Most of the people in Scripture who pondered the problem of evil in the world started from a different premise—the wicked enjoy long life and freedom from trouble, while the righteous suffer much and die young (Pss. 37; 73; Jer. 12:1-4). Zophar was deliberately blocking out a lot of data to prove his point.

According to Zophar, the higher the wicked man climbs in his success, the farther down he will fall when his judgment comes. When he falls, he will go down the drain like his own dung; and people will ask, "Where is he?" (Job 20:6-7) He will vanish like a forgotten dream or like a night vision that cannot be called back (v. 8).

Not only will the wicked man's person and name vanish, but so will his wealth. After his death, the truth about his crimes will become known; and his children will have to use their inheritance to pay back the people their father has robbed. Their father was still in "youthful vigor" when he died (v. 11, NIV), but now he lies lifeless in the grave. According to Zophar, the wicked die young, when they least expect it.

When you survey both sacred and secular history, you discover that there are no ironclad rules that govern when either the wicked or the righteous will die. Generally speaking, people who ignore God's laws are more vulnerable to problems that could lead to an early death. Sexual promiscuity, the use of narcotics (including alcohol and tobacco), and a reckless lifestyle can all help shorten a person's life; *but there is no guarantee that this will happen.* It's amazing how some godless people live to an old age. Perhaps this is the grace of God in giving them time to repent.

Zophar was not talking about the natural consequences of a wicked life, but the judgment of God on sinners. Zophar and his two friends were certain that Job was a hypocrite, that his pious life was only a veneer to cover his secret sins. In his second speech, Eliphaz will even name some of the sins that Job committed! (22:5-9) But God does not always judge hypocrites immediately, and the death of a young person is no evidence that he or she was a hypocrite.

The godly Scottish Presbyterian minister Robert Murray McCheyne died was he was only twenty-nine years old, and missionary William Whiting Borden ("Borden of Yale") was only twenty-five years old when he died in Egypt. David Brainerd, saintly missionary to the Native Americans, was twenty-nine when he died. According to Zophar, these men must have been guilty of secret sin, and God took them at an early age.

Their pleasure is temporary (Job 20:12-19). Zophar uses *eating* as his basic image here. The wicked man enjoys sin the way people enjoy food, keeping it in his mouth where he can "taste it" before swallowing it. In fact, he enjoys sin so much, he can't make himself swallow it! But eventually that delicious food in his mouth becomes poison in his system, and he becomes ill and vomits everything up. While enjoying his sin, he hasn't noticed that he's been bitten by a poisonous viper and is destined for death. In other words, sin carries with it both enjoyment and punishment; and if you want the one, you must also accept the other. The pleasures of sin are only for a season (Heb. 11:25).

But God's judgment involves much more: the wicked man not only gets sick from his sin, but he does not enjoy the everyday blessings of life (Job 20:17). "He will not see the streams, the rivers flowing with honey and cream" (NKJV). The land of Canaan was a land "flowing with milk and honey" (Ex. 3:8; Lev. 20:24). Milk and honey were staples, not luxuries; and a land "flowing with milk and honey" would be productive and able to support the people. But the wicked man has lost his taste for basic foods, and nothing satisfies him anymore. His taste for sin has ruined his enjoyment of the fundamental blessings of life.

Using the image of *eating*, Zophar has made two points: what the wicked man swallows will make him sick and will take away his desire for the good things of life. He makes a third point in Job 20:18-19: the wicked man will not be able to enjoy (swallow down) some of the things he labored for. Because he acquired his wealth through sinning, that wealth will not satisfy him.

This certainly has been reflected in the lives of many people who have rejected Christ and devoted themselves to the pleasures of sin. The more they indulge, the more they crave; and the more they satisfy that craving, the less they enjoy. The less they enjoy, the more they have to sin in order to recapture the old thrills; and the more they sin, the more they destroy their ability to enjoy anything. To change the image, they have "blown all their fuses"; and the machinery of life no longer functions as it once did.

Their death is painful (Job 20:20-29). Not even his riches will be able to prevent death from coming to the wicked man (Job 20:20; see Ps. 49). While he is enjoying his prosperity, the wicked man will experience distress, misery, and God's burning anger. God will "rain down His blows upon him" (Job 20:23, NIV). The evil man will try to run away, but God will come at him with a sword and shoot at him with a bronze-tipped arrow that will pierce him.

At this point in his speech, Zophar starts to sound like Bildad (Job 18). He describes the wicked man trying to escape God's judgment. The arrows come at him as he runs through the darkness, and the fire falls around him. Then a flood catches up with him and destroys everything. But that's not the end: The wicked man is finally dragged into court where heaven and earth testify against him and find him guilty (20:27).

2. The actual end of the wicked man (Job 21:1-34)

After appealing once more for their understanding and sympathy (Job 21:1-6), Job replied to Zophar's statements and refuted each of them. Job stated that, from his point of view, it appears that the wicked have long lives (vv. 7-16), they are not often sent calamity (vv. 17-21), and the death of the wicked is no different from the death of other men (vv. 22-34). Point by point, Job took Zophar's speech and shredded it into bits.

But first, listen to Job's appeal to his friends that they try to understand how he feels. "If you really want to console me, just keep quiet and listen" (v. 2, paraphrase). The Greek philosopher Zeno said, "The reason why we have two ears and only one mouth is that we may listen the more and talk the less." The friends thought their words would encourage Job, but he said that their silence would encourage him even more (13:3).

Job pointed out that his complaint was not against men but against God. Men had not caused his afflictions, and men could not take them away. If he was impatient, it was because God had not answered him (v. 3). The longer God waited, the worse Job's situation became. "Look at me and be astonished; clap your hand over your mouth" (21:5, NIV).

As Job contemplated what he was about to say, it stirred him to the depths (v. 6). This was no speech from "off the top of his head," for it had to do with the basic facts of life and death. If Job's friends were in his situation, they would see things differently and *say* things differently.

The life of the wicked may be long (Job 21:7-16). In contrast to Zophar's text (20:5), Job said, "Why do the wicked still live, continue on, also become very powerful?" (21:7, NASB) They have security on every side: their children and homes are safe (vv. 8-9, 11-12), their business prospers (v. 10), and they have long lives in which to enjoy their prosperity (v. 13).

They also have many descendants who share the family wealth and enjoy it. The death of the wicked is sudden; they don't linger in agony and long for deliverance. Of course, Job's situation was just the opposite: His family had been destroyed, his wealth was gone, and he was suffering greatly as he waited for death to come.

But the saddest thing about the wicked is the way they leave God out of their lives *and still prosper* (vv. 14-15). They want nothing to do with the Lord; in fact, they say to Him, "Get away from us! Leave us alone!" They refuse to pray to the Lord, obey Him, or give Him credit for their success. This is the philosophy of most unsaved people today; you might call it "practical atheism" (see Ps. 10). God is not in their thoughts, let alone in their plans (James 4:13-17). They are self-sufficient as they do what they want to do, and they do it "their way." Jesus described such a person in Luke 12:13-21.

Job hastened to say that this was not *his* philosophy of life. "But I refuse even to deal with people like that" (Job 21:16, TLB). The wicked take credit for their wealth, but Job acknowledged that everything comes from God (1:21). How, then, can Job's three friends classify him with the wicked?

Before considering Job's second point, we must face the disturbing fact that too many professed Christians actually admire and envy the lifestyle of the rich and famous. In one of his books, Dr. Kenneth Chafin tells about a pastor and deacon who were visiting prospects and stopped at a beautiful suburban home. The lawn looked like it was manicured, and two expensive cars sat in the driveway. Furthermore, the pastor and deacon could see the man of the house comfortably seated in his spacious living room, watching television. Everything about the place reeked of affluence. The deacon turned to his pastor and asked, "What kind of good news do we have for this fellow?"

In over forty years of ministry, I have performed many weddings and watched many young Christian couples get started in their homes. What a joy it has been to see homes where couples set the right priorities and resist the temptation to "follow the crowd" and live for material possessions. Unfortunately, some have lost their spiritual vision and succeeded in this world—without acknowledging the Lord. Alas, they have their reward.

The wicked do not often experience calamity? (Job 21:17-21) "Yea, the light of the wicked shall be put out," Bildad affirmed (18:5); but Job asked, "How often does that happen?" How often do you actually see God's anger displayed against the godless people of the world? "How often are they like straw before the wind, like chaff swept away by a gale?" (21:18, NIV) The wicked seem to be secure in this world, while the righteous suffer (but see Ps. 73).

But if God doesn't judge the wicked, He will judge their children (Job 21:19). Zophar had argued that point (20:10), and so had Eliphaz (5:4). Of course, both of them were aiming at Job, who had lost all of his children. "But what kind of judgment is that?" asked Job. "If a man lives in sin, let him suffer for his sin. After he dies, why should he care about what happens to his family? In Sheol, he will never know what is happening on earth."

Scripture makes it clear that the fathers are not punished for the sins of the children or the children for the sins of the fathers (Jer. 31:29-30; Ezek. 18:1ff). Certainly parents may be deeply hurt by the sins of their children, and children may suffer from the *consequences* of their parents' sins, but the judgment of God is always just (Deut. 24:16). It was cruel for the three friends to suggest that Job's sins had caused the death of his children.

Zophar had said that the life of a wicked man was brief, but Job refuted him by affirming that wicked people often live a long time. Zophar claimed that the pleasures of the wicked were temporary because God's judgment suddenly fell upon them, but Job asked, "How often have you seen that happen?" Now Job answers Zophar's third argument that the death of the wicked is painful.

The wicked die just like other people (Job 21:22-34). Life and death are in the hands of God, so what is mere man that he should teach God or claim to be able to explain God's ways? (v. 22) God will ask Job a similar question when He finally appears and gives Job his long-awaited opportunity to defend himself. Instead of Job questioning God, it will be God who questions Job and humbles Job with His questions!

Observation tells Job that some people die when they are in the fullness of life and apparently in excellent health, while others die after long and painful illnesses. Some people enjoy a long and happy life while others spend their days in misery, *but death is the same for all of them.* Strictly speaking, there is no such thing as "infant death" or "tragic death" or "unexpected death" because *death is death no matter when or how it comes.* The rich man dies, the poor man dies; the believer dies, the unbeliever dies; and "side by side they lie in the dust, and worms cover them both" (v. 26, NIV). Of course, Job is talking about the *physical* side of death and not the *spiritual.* When death comes, it obviously makes a great deal of difference *in the next life* whether or not the person had faith in Jesus Christ (Heb. 9:27).

Many people—including some Christian believers—hesitate to speak about death in general or their own death in particular. They have hospitalization and life insurance, but they prefer to avoid the subject and act as though death were not coming. "The idea of death, the fear of it, haunts the human animal like nothing else," wrote sociologist Ernest Becker. "It is a mainspring of human activity—activity designed largely to avoid the fatality of death, to overcome it by denying in some way that it is the final destiny for man" (*The Denial of Death*, Free Press p. ix).

"Behold, I know your thoughts," Job told his friends (Job 21:27). He could tell that his speech had not convinced them, and he knew just what they were going to say when he finished speaking—exactly what they had said before! In verse 28 he quoted two of their statements that he had already refuted (see 18:13-21 and 20:20-29), but he expected to hear similar statements again.

Job asked his friends if they had ever investigated the situation in places other than their own homeland. As Dorothy Sayers wrote, "There's nothing you can't prove if your outlook is only sufficiently limited." He asked them, "Have you never questioned those who travel?" (21:29, NIV) People who travel are usually not provincial in their outlook but have wide experience in the things of the world. With all of their wisdom, Job's three friends might still be narrow in their outlook because they haven't seen what life is like in other places. If Job's friends inquired of well-traveled people, they would learn that in every part of the world, wicked people seem to escape the calamities that fall on the righteous.

Then Job became very personal and asked his friends, "If you really believe that the wicked are destined for an early death, *have you ever warned them?* Have you ever denounced them to their face?" (v. 31, paraphrase) If his friends had replied, "No, we have never talked to the wicked about their future," then Job could have said, "Then why are you warning *a righteous man* about his future?" How inconsistent can you get?

Job's closing words in 21:34 let the three friends know that he had no confidence in what they said. Their comfort was in vain ("nonsense," NIV), and their answers were nothing but falsehood. The Hebrew word translated "falsehood" means "a deliberate violation of God's Law, an act of treachery." It is often translated "trespass." When the three friends attacked Job, they were breaking faith and trespassing against God. Instead of helping Job, they were leading him astray.

I have a friend who prays daily, "Lord, help me today not to add to anybody's burdens."

It's too bad Bildad and Zophar and Eliphaz didn't pray that prayer!

Perhaps all of us should start praying it!

INTERLUDE

If you want to be an encouragement to hurting people, try to see things through their eyes. Be humble enough to admit that there might be other points of view. Job's three friends had a narrow experience of life. They held fast to their dogmatic assumptions and refused to budge. In a letter to some people who disagreed with him, Oliver Cromwell wrote, "I beseech you, in the bowels of Christ, think it possible you may be mistaken."

Someone has defined fanatics as "people who can't change their minds and won't change the subject." Samuel Johnson once said of a man, "That man has only one idea, and it is wrong."

There is always something new to learn about God, the Bible, people, and life. Let's be good learners—and good listeners!

EIGHT

"The God of Israel, the Savior, is sometimes a God that hides Himself, but never a God that absents Himself; sometimes in the dark, but never at a distance."

Matthew Henry

Order in the Court!

What should have been an encouraging discussion among friends had become an angry and painful debate. Instead of trying to calm things down, Eliphaz assumed the office of prosecuting attorney and turned the debate into a trial. It was three against one as Job sat on the ash heap and listened to his friends lie about him. According to the Jewish Talmud, "The slanderous tongue kills three: the slandered, the slanderer, and him who listens to the slander." At the ash heap in Uz, it was death all around!

1. Three false accusations (Job 22:1-30)

Like any effective attorney, Eliphaz had the case well in hand and his brief all prepared. He made three serious accusations against Job: he is a sinner (Job 22:1-11), he is hiding his sins (vv. 12-20), and he must confess his sins and repent before God can help him (vv. 21-30).

Job is a sinner (Job 22:1-11). Eliphaz can't resist shooting a sarcastic barb at Job. "Is it for your piety that He [God] rebukes you and brings charges against you?" (v. 4, NIV) Courts don't try people for their righteousness but for their lawlessness! Therefore, since God has sent terrible judgments upon Job, he must be guilty of sin. "Is not your wickedness great? Are not your sins endless?" (v. 5, NIV) But Eliphaz missed the point that Job had been making: "Why does God send the punishment *before He arrests me, reads the indictment, and conducts the trial?"* It all seemed unfair.

Eliphaz first accused Job of the sin of *pride* (vv. 1-3). Job was acting as though his character and conduct were important to God and beneficial to Him in some way. Eliphaz's theology centered around a distant God who was the Judge of the world but not the Friend of sinners.

But Job's character and conduct *were* important to God, *for God was using Job to silence the devil.* Neither Job nor his three friends knew God's hidden plan, but Job had faith to believe that God was achieving some purpose in his life and would one day vindicate him. Furthermore, the character and behavior of God's people *are* important to the Lord because His people bring Him either joy or sorrow (1 Thes. 4:1; Heb. 11:5; Gen. 6:5-6; Ps. 37:23). He is not a passive, distant God who does not identify with His people but the God who delights in them as they delight in Him (Ps. 18:19; Isa. 63:9; Heb. 4:14-16).

As God's children, we should follow the example of Jesus who said, "I do always those things that please Him" (John 8:29). Then the Father will be able to say of us as He said of Jesus, "This is My beloved Son, in whom I am well pleased" (Matt. 3:17).

Along with pride, Eliphaz accused Job of *covetousness* (Job 22:6). He was a greedy man who abused people to acquire more wealth. He used his power and reputation (v. 8) to intimidate people and rob them. In the Mosaic Law, a creditor could take security from a debtor but not anything that would jeopardize his work, his health, or his dignity as a human being (Ex. 22:25-27; Deut. 24:10-13). Eliphaz accused Job of taking security from his brothers when none was needed, and he left people naked because he took their clothing from them until they paid their debts!

Eliphaz didn't even live in Job's territory, so how would he know how Job had treated people in his business dealings? Had some of Job's enemies passed these stories to Eliphaz? If so, he should have investigated the charges before announcing them publicly. The whole thing was pure fabrication, a feeble attempt to discredit a godly man who had helped many people (Job 29:11-17).

Job's third great sin was *lack of mercy and compassion* (22:7-9), which was a sin of omission. No wonder the Lord was not answering Job's prayers! "Whoever shuts his ears to the cry of the poor will also cry himself and not be heard" (Prov. 21:13). Job had turned away the weary, the hungry, the widows, and the orphans, instead of sharing with them out of his rich resources. Since showing hospitality is one of the first laws of the East, Job's sin was especially heinous.

Throughout Scripture, God shows a great concern for the poor, especially widows and orphans, and expresses anger at those who oppress the poor and exploit them (Ex. 22:22; Deut. 24:17, 26:12). The prophets scathingly denounced leaders, both political and religious, who oppressed the needy and robbed the poor (Isa. 1:17; Jer. 7:6; 22:1-4; Amos 4:1; 5:11; 8:4-10). Jesus had a special concern for the poor (Luke 4:16-19; Matt. 11:5), and the early church followed His example (Gal. 2:10; James 1:27; 2:1-9; Acts 6:1; 1 Tim. 5:1-16). The church *today* needs to follow that example.

Eliphaz clinched his first point with evidence anybody could see: Job was suffering great trials, which were the consequences of his many sins (Job 22:10-11). Why else would he be in darkness, danger, and the depths of suffering? This was the hand of God indicating that Job was a godless man.

The people who were standing around and listening to the

discussion must have been shocked when they heard these accusations against their neighbor Job. They must have looked at each other and asked, "How can this be? Why didn't we know about Job's wickedness?" Eliphaz's next point answered their question.

Job is hiding his sins (Job 22:12-20). In other words, Job was a hypocrite, a statement that was made—or hinted at— more than once since the discussion began. "The hypocrite's hope shall perish," said Bildad (8:13). "For the congregation of hypocrites shall be desolate," said Eliphaz (15:34). And Zophar said, "The joy of the hypocrite [is] but for a moment" (20:5).

A hypocrite is not a person who fails to reach his desired spiritual goals, because all of us fail in one way or another. A hypocrite is a person who doesn't even try to reach any goals, *but he makes people think that he has.* His profession and his practice never meet. The Puritan preacher Stephen Charnock said, "It is a sad thing to be Christians at a supper, heathens in our shops, and devils in our closets."

Eliphaz advised Job to *look up* (22:12-14) and realize that nobody can hide anything from God. A hypocrite encourages himself in his sin by saying, "The Lord doesn't know and doesn't care" (see Ps. 10). But God sees and knows all things, and the hypocrite can't hide his sins from the Lord. God may not judge immediately, but eventually judgment will fall.

Then Eliphaz advised Job to *look back* (vv. 15-18) and remember what has happened to sinners in the past. Job had made it clear that he had nothing to do with "the counsel of the wicked" (21:16), but Eliphaz accused him of walking on that very path (22:15). History shows that hypocrites can hide their sins for only so long, and then their sins find them out. God is not only patient with them, but He is good to them and fills their houses with good things (v. 18). The fact that

Job was a very wealthy man was evidence of God's kindness and not Job's righteousness.

Poor Job! No matter which way he turned or how he tried to reason with his accusers, he was wasting his time and energy. First they said that God blesses the righteous and punishes the wicked, and now Eliphaz claims that God blesses the hypocrite and fills his house with good things!

The tragedy of hypocrisy is not only that God sends judgment, but that hypocrisy brings its own judgment. It destroys character; and when character is gone, when the salt has lost its flavor (see Matt. 5:13), what does a person have left?

It has well been said that the highest reward for a faithful life is not what you get for it but what you become by it. Bishop Brooke Westcott said, "Great occasions do not make heroes or cowards; they simply unveil them to the eyes of men. Silently and imperceptibly, as we wake or sleep, we grow strong or we grow weak, and at last some crisis shows what we have become."

Job must repent of his sins (Job 22:21-30). Eliphaz was sincere in his appeal to Job, just as Zophar was sincere when he asked Job to return to God (11:13-20). "Submit to God and be at peace with Him; in this way prosperity will come to you" (22:21, NIV). The word translated "prosperity" means "good of every kind." Of course, a hypocrite should return to God, not just to get out of trouble and restore his or her fortunes, but to please and glorify God in the rebuilding of character and service.

What does it mean to "submit to God"? It means to stop fighting God and accept His terms of peace (James 4:1-10). It also means to listen to His Word and obey what God says (Job 22:22). A sinner must put away sin (v. 23) and make God his greatest treasure (v. 25); he must pray and seek God's face (v. 27).

What does God promise to those who repent and return to

Him? God will restore them (v. 23) and make Himself precious to them (v. 25) so that all their delight will be in the Lord and not in earthly wealth or pleasure (v. 26). God will answer their prayers and enable them to do His will (v. 27) as He gives direction and light (v. 28). Because they are restored to fellowship with God, they can help others who have fallen (vv. 29-30).

Eliphaz says some excellent things in this appeal, but he says them to the wrong man. When we get to the end of the book, we will discover that it is Eliphaz and his two friends who are out of fellowship with God. They will need Job to intercede for them so they can be restored (42:7-10).

If you were Job, how would you respond to this appeal?

2. Three bitter complaints (Job 23–24)

Instead of arguing with his friends, or compromising his integrity by giving in to Eliphaz's appeal, Job ignores them completely and speaks to and about the Lord. Job has already made it clear that his dispute was not with men but with God, and he emphasizes this fact in his speech.

We may paraphrase Job 23:2, "My complaint today is bitter, and I have to keep a heavy hand on myself to keep from doing nothing but groaning." Job's three friends did not understand how much discipline Job needed just to be able to talk with them. Instead of giving in to his pain and doing nothing but groan, Job sought to master his pain and not give in to self-pity. The next time you visit somebody in pain, keep in mind that suffering drains a person's energy and makes great demands on his strength and patience.

Job said that he had three complaints against the Lord.

"God is hiding from me" (Job 23:1-12). "Oh, that I knew where I might find Him, that I might come even to His seat [throne]!" (v. 3) This was another appeal to meet God in court and have a fair trial. Job was prepared to state his case,

present his arguments, and let God give the verdict. Job was confident that, despite God's great power as a Lawgiver, he would win his case for he was an upright man, and God could not condemn the upright in heart. "There an upright man could present his case before Him, and I would be delivered forever from my judge" (v. 7, NIV).

But how does a mere man go about finding God? If Job went forward or backward (east or west), to the left or to the right (north or south), he could not see God or even catch a quick glimpse of Him. Of course, God is present everywhere (Ps. 139:7-12); but Job wanted a *personal* meeting with God. He had questions to ask and arguments to present!

God knew where Job was—in the furnace! (Job 23:10) But it was a furnace of God's appointment, not because of Job's sin; and God would use Job's affliction to purify him and make him a better man. This is not the only answer to the question, "Why do the righteous suffer?" but it is one of the best, and it can bring the sufferer great encouragement.

Scripture often uses the image of a furnace to describe God's purifying ministry through suffering. "See, I have refined you, though not as silver; I have tested you in the furnace of affliction" (Isa. 48:10, NIV). Israel's suffering in Egypt was like that of iron in a smelting furnace (Deut. 4:20), and her later disciplines were also a "furnace experience." "For You, O God, tested us; You refined us like silver" (Ps. 66:10, NIV). This image is used in 1 Peter 1:6-7 and 4:12 of believers going through persecution.

When God puts His own people into the furnace, He keeps His eye on the clock and His hand on the thermostat. He knows how long and how much. We may question why He does it to begin with, or why He doesn't turn down the heat or even turn it off; but our questions are only evidences of unbelief. Job 23:10 is the answer: "But He knows the way that I take; when He has tested me, I shall come come forth as gold" (NKJV). *Gold does not fear the fire.* The furnace can only make the gold purer and brighter.

It's important to note that Job's life was pleasing to God *before he went into the furnace* (vv. 11-12). Eliphaz had warned Job to receive God's words and obey them (22:22), but Job had already been doing that. God's Word was his *guide* as he walked the path of life, and he was careful not to go on any detours. But even more, God's Word was his *nourishment* that was more important to him than his daily meals. Like Jeremiah (Jer. 15:16) and Jesus (Matt. 4:4; John 4:31-34), Job found in God's Word the only food that satisfied his inner person. (See Pss. 1:2; 119:103; 1 Peter 2:1-3.)

Some people go into the furnace of affliction, and it burns them; others go in, and the experience purifies them. What makes the difference? *Their attitude toward the Word of God and the will of God.* If we are nourished by the Word and submit to His will, the furnace experience, painful as it may be, will refine us and make us better. But if we resist God's will and fail to feed on His truth, the furnace experience will only burn us and make us bitter.

Job had a second complaint.

"God is frightening me" (Job 23:13-17). "But He stands alone, and who can oppose Him? He does whatever He pleases" (v. 13, NIV). Job had no other gods to turn to for help, and no way to oppose God or change His mind. God runs the universe by decree, not by consensus or democratic vote. His thoughts and ways are far above ours, but He knows what is best, and we must accept His will and rejoice in it (Isa. 55:8-11).

Those who resist or deny the sovereignty of God rob themselves of peace and courage. "There is no attribute of God more comforting to His children than the doctrine of divine sovereignty," said Charles Haddon Spurgeon. "On the other hand, there is no doctrine more hated by worldlings."

Why? Because the human heart is proud and does not want to submit to Almighty God. People want to "do their own thing" and "do it their way," rather than find delight in doing the will of God.

If this doctrine is such a source of strength, then why was Job so frightened when he thought about the sovereignty of God? It was because he suffered so much and wondered what Almighty God would send to him next. It's one thing to submit to God when you can see His face and hear His voice in His Word. But when, like Job, you are in darkness and pain, it is easy to "fall apart" and become frightened. "He carries out His decree against me, and many such plans He still has in store" (Job 23:14, NIV). What will happen next?

But Job 23:14 must be contrasted with Jeremiah 29:11 — " 'For I know the plans I have for you,' declares the Lord, 'plans to prosper you and not to harm you, plans to give you hope and a future' " (NIV). *The future is your friend when Jesus Christ is your Lord, and you need not be afraid.* Psychologist Rollo May writes, "The most effective way to ensure the value of the future is to confront the present courageously and constructively." And the best way to do that is to submit to the Lord and realize that He is in control. "Hallelujah! For the Lord God omnipotent reigneth" (Rev. 19:6).

"God perplexes me" (Job 24:1-25). This entire chapter focuses on the seeming injustices that God permits in this world. Job opens his speech by asking in effect, "Why doesn't God have specific days to hold court? Then I could attend and tell Him what I think of the way He is running the world!"

Job starts with *injustices in the country* (vv. 1-11), and then moves to *crimes in the city* (vv. 12-17). He closes his speech with *a curse on the wicked* (vv. 18-25). If God won't judge them, Job will!

(1) Injustices in the country (vv. 1-11). For the most part, no walls or fences separated the farm lands; each family had its

plot, and people respected the landmarks ("boundary stones," NIV; see Deut. 19:14; Prov. 22:28; 23:10). God promised to curse those who moved the landmarks and stole property (Deut. 27:17), but wicked men did it just the same.

But they didn't stop there. They not only claimed the land, but also the animals that grazed on the land! They took flocks and donkeys and oxen from widows and orphans and left them in poverty. Job 24:5-11 gives one of the most graphic pictures of the plight of the poor found anywhere in the Bible. See them foraging for food like wild animals in the desert (vv. 5-6), freezing because they have no clothing (v. 7), drenched by the rain because they have no houses to live in (v. 8), weeping because their children have been snatched from their arms until they pay their debts (v. 9), and forced to work for the rich and yet not allowed to eat any of the food that they harvest (vv. 10-11). Even the oxen are permitted to eat the grain that they thresh! (Deut. 25:4)

"Now," says Job to his friends, "if God judges the wicked, why hasn't He judged those who have treated the poor so unjustly and inhumanely?"

(2) Crimes in the city (vv. 12-17). Job begins with *murders* (vv. 12-14); he hears the groans of the wounded and sees the death of the innocent. On the average, 60 Americans are murdered every day, a total of nearly 22,000 people annually. That's like wiping out an entire city about the size of Fairbanks, Alaska; or El Cerrito, California; or Augusta, Maine. Some of these murderers are never identified, arrested, or convicted; and Job says, "But God charges no one with wrongdoing" (v. 12, NIV). Job had never murdered anybody, yet his friends said he was under the judgment of God!

In verse 15, Job mentions *sexual sins,* which are certainly rampant in some parts of our cities. The adulterer and the rapist wait for the darkness before they sneak out to satisfy their desires. Also waiting for the darkness is *the thief,* who breaks into houses (vv. 16-17). "There is crime in the city," said Job, "and God seems to be doing nothing about it."

(3) A curse on the wicked (vv. 18-25). This passage may be seen as a *description,* telling what will happen to the wicked (KJV, NIV, NASB); or it may be interpreted as a *denunciation,* a curse on the wicked (NKJV). I think it refers to Job's personal curse on the wicked, who seem to escape judgment.

Job's malediction can be summarized like this: "May the wicked vanish like foam on the water or snow that melts in the heat of the sun (vv. 18-19). May they be forgotten by everyone, even their own mothers, as they rot in the grave (v. 20). May their wives be barren and give them no heirs (v. 21). May their sense of security and success vanish quickly as they are brought low, mowed down like wheat in the harvest" (vv. 22-24).

"Now," says Job to his three critics, "if what I've said is not true, prove me wrong!" (v. 25) But they never did.

Job is to be commended for seeing somebody else's troubles besides his own and for expressing a holy anger against sin and injustice. Too often, personal suffering can make us selfish and even blind us to the needs of others, but Job was concerned that God help others who were hurting. His three friends were treating the problem of suffering in far too abstract a fashion, and Job tried to get them to see *hurting people* and not just philosophical problems. Jesus had the same problem with the Jewish lawyer who wanted to discuss "neighborliness," but not discover who his neighbor was and then try to help him (Luke 10:25-37).

Injustices in society cause a good deal of pain in people's lives, and we should certainly do all we can to uphold the law and promote justice. But those who make the laws and those who enforce them are only human and can't deal with everything perfectly. One of these days, the Lord Jesus Christ will return, judge the wicked, and establish His righteous kingdom. Till He comes, we will have to accept the reality of evil in this world and keep praying, "Even so, come, Lord Jesus" (Rev. 22:20).

"Every year makes me tremble at the daring with which people speak of spiritual things."

Bishop Brooke F. Westcott

How Faint a Whisper!

Bildad's speech in Job 25 is the shortest in the book and focuses on God's power (vv. 1-3) and justice (vv. 4-6). It is disturbing to see how Job's friends speak so knowingly about God when, in the end, God revealed that they really didn't know what they were talking about. Too often, those who say the most about God know the least about God.

God's power is inherent in His nature (vv. 1-3): He has all dominion and fear ("awe") and reigns sovereignly in the heavens. He has everything under control and sees what is going on in all places. His army of angels is at His command and ready to obey His will. Who can resist Him?

God's justice is the outworking of His holy nature (vv. 4-6), for "God is light, and in Him is no darkness at all" (1 John 1:5). Since God is holy and just, how can mere man claim to be righteous before Him? (Remember, Job was holding fast to his integrity and refusing to confess that his sins had brought God's judgment on him.) Since man is born of woman, he is born with a sinful nature (Ps. 51:5). In the East, the moon and stars shine with great brilliance; but even they are not pure in God's sight. How can a mere man claim to be righteous before God, man who is nothing but a maggot and a worm? (See Job 4:17-18; 8:20; 9:2.) Now, we listen to Job's reply.

1. Job acknowledges God's power (Job 26)

Before magnifying God's great power in the universe, Job first rebuked Bildad for giving him no help (Job 26:1-4). Job had no power, but Bildad didn't make him stronger. According to his friends, Job lacked wisdom; yet Bildad didn't share one piece of wisdom or insight. "Who has helped you utter these words? And whose spirit spoke from your mouth?" (v. 4, NIV) If Bildad's words had come from God, then they would have done Job good; for Job had been crying out for God to speak to him. The conclusion is that Bildad's words came from Bildad, and that's why they did Job no good.

Then Job extolled the greatness of God (vv. 5-13). God sees everything, even the realm of the dead (vv. 5-6). Job used three different names for the place of the dead: the waters, Sheol, and "destruction" (Abaddon, Rev. 9:11). If God sees what's going on in the world of the dead, then surely He knows what is happening in the world of the living!

God not only sees everything, but He made everything and controls it (Job 26:7-13). Job began his hymn of praise with a statement about God's power in *the heavens* (vv. 7-9), and he described the earth with remarkable scientific accuracy (v. 7). God also controls the clouds and the rain.

Job then moved his attention to *the earth* (vv. 10-11) and praised God for marking out the horizon where the sun rises and sets. He is the God who controls day and night, land and water. The "pillars of heaven" is a poetic phrase for the mountains; they rest on earth, but they seem to hold up the heavens. All God has to do is speak, and the mountains tremble (9:6).

The last stanza of Job's hymn centers on God's power in *the waters* (26:12-13). God can stir up the sea or still it as He desires, and He has power over sea creatures ("Rahab" and "the gliding serpent," NIV). He can blow the storm clouds away and clear the sky after the storm.

The three friends must have listened impatiently because they already knew the things Job was talking about; *but they hadn't drawn the right conclusion from them.* Because they saw God's handiwork in nature, they thought they knew all about God; and therefore they could explain God to Job.

Job said that just the opposite was true. "Behold, these are the fringes of His ways; and how faint a word we hear of Him! But His mighty thunder, who can understand?" (v. 14, NASB) What we see of God in creation is but the fringes of His ways, and what we hear is but a whisper of His power! You may read The Book of Nature carefully and still have a great deal more to learn about God. Knowing a few facts about the creation of God is not the same as knowing truths about the God of Creation.

The fourteenth-century British spiritual writer Richard Rolle said, "He truly knows God perfectly that finds Him incomprehensible and unable to be known." The more we learn about God, the more we discover how much more there is to know! Beware of people who claim to know all about God, for their claim is proof they know neither God nor themselves.

2. Job questions God's justice (Job 27)

Bildad had made it clear that since God is holy, no man can stand righteous in His sight (Job 25:4-6). The corollary to this proposition is that God is obligated to punish people for their sins; otherwise, He would not be a righteous God. If Job is suffering, it must be that Job is sinning.

Job takes an oath (Job 27:1-6). Once again, Job stood fast in affirming his integrity (10:1-7; 13:13-19; 19:23-27; 23:2-7); but this time, he gave an oath: "As God lives" (27:2). Among

Eastern people in that day, taking an oath was a serious matter. It was like inviting God to kill you if what you said was not true. Job was so sure of himself that he was willing to take that chance.

Job also repeated his charge that God was not treating him fairly ("[He] has denied me justice," v. 2, NIV). Job had asked God to declare the charges against him, but the heavens had been silent. Job had called for an umpire to bring him and God together, but no umpire had been provided.

So, Job declared that, as long as he lived, he would defend himself and maintain his integrity. He would not lie just to please his friends or to "bribe" God into restoring his fortunes. (Satan would have rejoiced at that!) Job had to live with his conscience ("heart," v. 6) no matter what his friends said or his God did to him.

Job utters a curse (Job 27:7-10). In the East, it was not enough for accused people simply to affirm their innocence; they also felt compelled to call down the wrath of God on those who said they were guilty. Job's words remind us of the "imprecatory psalms" (Pss. 58, 69, 137, etc.) in that they are a prayer for God's judgment on his enemies.

Who were Job's enemies? Anybody who agreed with Job's three friends that he was guilty of sin and deserved to be punished by God. While this conversation had been going on, many people had likely gathered around the ash heap and listened to the debate; and most of them probably sided with Bildad, Zophar, and Eliphaz. Job could see the spectators nod their heads in agreement with his friends, and he knew that he was outnumbered.

Job's words sound cruel to us, especially in light of what we are taught about forgiving our enemies by both Jesus (Matt. 5:38-48) and Paul (Rom. 12:17-21). But Job lived even before the Mosaic Law was given, let alone the Sermon on the Mount; and we must not expect him to manifest the kind of spirit that was seen in Jesus (Luke 23:34) and Stephen (Acts 7:60).

However, in the sight of God, *Job was right*. God had *twice* declared before the court of heaven that Job was "a blameless and upright man, one who fears God and shuns evil" (Job 1:8; 2:3, NKJV). Therefore, Job's enemies were wrong; and Job had the right to ask God to vindicate him. In fact, *God was the only one who could prove Job right and his enemies wrong*. Where else could Job turn for help?

The three friends had repeatedly warned Job about the terrible destiny of the wicked, so Job threw their words right back at them. "May my enemies be like the wicked, my adversaries like the unjust" (27:7, NIV). Job saw his enemies experiencing great distress, calling out to God for help but getting no answer, and then being suddenly cut off by death. But isn't that the very judgment Job's friends predicted for him *and probably hoped would come?*

Bildad had affirmed that God is just and punishes those who disobey Him. But this does not mean that everybody who suffers is being punished for his or her sins. Sometimes we suffer because of the sins of others (e.g., Joseph) or because God is keeping us from sin (e.g., Paul in 2 Cor. 12). Jesus suffered, not for His own sins, for He had none, but for the sins of the world (1 Peter 2:22-24; 3:18); and because of His suffering and death, sinners can believe and receive eternal life.

Job teaches a lesson (Job 27:11-23). "I will teach you about the power of God" (27:11, NIV), says Job; and he describes God's judgment of the wicked. On the day when God vindicates Job, this is what will happen to his enemies.

They will die, and their widows will not mourn for them, a terrible insult in the Eastern world. Their children will be slain by the sword or the plague; and if any survive, they will spend the rest of their lives begging for something to eat.

The wicked will lie down rich and wake up poor. Their silver and expensive clothing will be gone. Their houses will be destroyed like cocoons (or spiders' webs), or like the temporary shacks of the watchmen in the fields. The death of the wicked will not be peaceful. Terrors will come in at night like a flood and carry him away. Even if the wicked try to flee, the storm will follow them and destroy them.

You can recognize in this description many of the images that Job's friends used in their "judgment" speeches against him. Job did this deliberately to remind them that they had better be careful what they say *lest they declare their own punishment.* "Judge not, that you be not judged. For with what judgment you judge, you will be judged; and with the same measure you use, it will be measured back to you" (Matt. 7:1-2, NKJV).

Scripture records several instances where the judgment planned by an enemy was brought home to that enemy by the Lord. Pharaoh ordered the newborn Jewish boys to be drowned, and his own army was drowned in the Red Sea (Ex. 1:15-22; 14:23-31). Haman built a gallows on which to hang Mordecai, but Haman and his sons were hanged there instead (Es. 7:10; 9:25). Daniel's enemies tried to have him destroyed, but they and their families ended up in the lions' den in the place of Daniel (Dan. 6:24). (See Prov. 11:8.)

Scholars do not agree on the interpretation of Job 27:23. The NASB reads, "Men will clap their hands at him, and will hiss him from his place," and most translations agree with that; but the word *men* is not in the original text. It simply reads, "He claps his hands against him." Who is "he"? Elmer B. Smick in *The Expositor's Bible Commentary* suggests that it might be God, and that verse 23 should be connected with verse 13 where "God" is the subject of the sentence (vol. 4, p. 972). He translates verse 23, "He claps his hands against them and hisses at them from his dwelling [heaven]."

Whether God or men, there is rejoicing at the destruction of the wicked.

3. Job seeks God's wisdom (Job 28)

"But where shall wisdom be found?" (Job 28:12) "Where then does wisdom come from? Where does understanding dwell?" (v. 20, NIV) Job asked these questions because he was weary of the clichés and platitudes that his three friends were giving him in the name of "wisdom." His friends were sure that their words were pure gold, but Job concluded they were tinsel and trash. The three men had *knowledge*, but they lacked *wisdom*.

"Wisdom is the right use of knowledge," said Charles Spurgeon. "To know is not to be wise. Many men know a great deal, and are all the greater fools for it. There is no fool so great a fool as the knowing fool. But to know how to use knowledge is to have wisdom."

In this poem about wisdom, Job gives three answers to his question, "Where shall wisdom be found?"

You cannot mine wisdom (Job 28:1-11). Job takes us deep into the earth where brave men are mining gold, iron, copper, and precious stones. Precious metals and precious stones are often used in Scripture as symbols of wisdom (Prov. 2:1-10; 3:13-15; 8:10-21; 1 Cor. 3:12-23). Once you have found it, you must "refine" it in the furnace and "mint" it for practical use. Paul said that the opposite of God's wisdom is man's wisdom—"wood, hay, and stubble"—materials that are not beautiful, durable, or valuable (1 Cor. 3:12). You can find wood, hay, and stubble on the surface of the earth; but if you want real treasures, you must dig deep.

Job describes how men work hard and face great danger to find material wealth. They tunnel through hard rock and risk their lives to get rich. *Why will men and women not put that much effort into gaining God's wisdom?* The Word of God is like a deep mine, filled with precious treasures; but the believer must put forth effort to discover its riches. It takes careful reading and study, prayer, meditation, and obedience to mine the treasures of the Word of God; and the Holy Spirit of God is willing to assist us. Why are we so negligent when this great wealth lies so near at hand?

Though man can dig deep into the earth and find great wealth, though he can go places where birds and beasts would not dare to go, though he can even find the hidden sources of the great rivers, *man cannot find God's wisdom by mere human efforts.* It takes more than courage and native intelligence; it demands humility and spiritual perception.

The fact that a person succeeds admirably in one area of life doesn't mean he or she is qualified to speak about other areas of life. Advertisers use athletes to sell razors and automobiles, or actors and actresses to sell medicine. When famous scientists (who have never studied the Bible) speak authoritatively about spiritual things, their opinion is as valuable as that of any other untrained amateur theologian.

You cannot buy wisdom (Job 28:12-19). Modern society thinks that anything can be obtained or accomplished if only you have enough money. Government agencies ask for a bigger slice of the annual budget so they can do a better job of fighting crime, ending pollution, providing jobs, and building a better environment. While a certain amount of money is necessary to survive in modern society, money is not the do-all and be-all that the world says it is. It's good to enjoy the things money can buy (1 Tim. 6:17) *if you don't lose the things that money can't buy.*

In these verses, Job mentions gold five times, silver once, and names seven different precious stones; yet none of these treasures individually, nor all of them collectively, can purchase the wisdom of God. The real problem is that *man doesn't comprehend the price of wisdom and thinks he can get it cheaply* (Job 28:13). "[Wisdom] is more precious than rubies, and all the things you may desire cannot compare with her" (Prov. 3:15, NKJV). True wisdom is expensive. It is not received automatically just because you listen to a cassette tape, attend a seminar, or listen to a dynamic speaker.

Wisdom comes only from God (Job 28:20-28). Go as high as the birds can fly, and you won't find wisdom there. Go as deep as Abaddon and death, and wisdom is not there. Only God knows where to find wisdom, for God sees everything. (He doesn't have to dig into the earth to see what's there!) God has the wisdom to adjust the pressure of the wind and measure the amount of water in the atmosphere. If these proportions were changed, what disturbances in nature might result! God knows how to control the rain and guide the storm as it moves across the earth. Flashes of lightning and peals of thunder may seem arbitrary to us, but God controls even the lightning and thunder.

Job answers his where-is-wisdom question in Job 28:28: "Behold, the fear of the Lord, that is wisdom; and to depart from evil is understanding" (see Ps. 111:10; Prov. 1:7; 9:10). This was God's description of Job (Job 1:8; 2:3); so, in spite of what his friends said about him, *Job was a man of wisdom.*

What is "the fear of the Lord"? It is loving reverence for God, who He is, what He says, and what He does (Mal. 2:5-6). It is not a fear that paralyzes, but one that energizes. When you fear the Lord, you obey His commandments (Ecc. 12:13), walk in His ways (Deut. 8:6), and serve Him (Josh. 24:14). You are loyal to Him and give Him wholehearted service (2 Chron. 19:9). Like Job, when you fear the Lord, you depart from evil (Prov. 3:7-8). The "fear of the Lord" is the fear that conquers fear (Ps. 112); for if you fear God, you need not fear anyone else (Matt. 10:26-31).

So, the first step toward true wisdom is a reverent and respectful attitude toward God, which also involves a humble attitude toward ourselves. *Personal pride is the greatest barrier to spiritual wisdom.* "When pride comes, then comes shame; but with the humble is wisdom" (Prov. 11:2, NKJV).

The next step is to ask God for wisdom (James 1:5) and make diligent use of the means He gives us for securing His wisdom, especially knowing and doing the Word of God (Matt. 7:21-29). It is not enough merely to study; we must also obey what God tells us to do (John 7:17). As we walk by faith, we discover the wisdom of God in the everyday things of life. Spiritual wisdom is not abstract; it is very personal and very practical.

As we fellowship with other believers in the church and share with one another, we can learn wisdom. Reading the best books can also help us grow in wisdom and understanding. The important thing is that we focus on Christ, for He is our wisdom (1 Cor. 1:24) and in Him is hidden "all the treasures of wisdom and knowledge" (Col. 2:3). The better we know Christ and the more we become like Him, the more we will walk in wisdom and understand the will of the Lord. We must allow the Holy Spirit to open the eyes of our heart so we can see God in His Word and understand more of the riches we have in Christ (Eph. 1:15-23).

Job's speech is not yet finished. In the next three chapters, Job will review his life and then challenge God to either vindicate him or judge him. That will end the debate and usher in two new participants—Elihu and the Lord.

'As long as we want to be different from what God wants us to be at the time, we are only tormenting ourselves to no purpose."
Gerhart Tersteegen

"I Rest My Case!"

Job and his friends had shared three rounds of speeches, and now Job felt it was time for him to sum up his defense. The phrase "Moreover, Job continued his parable [discourse]" (Job 29:1) suggests that Job may have paused and waited for Zophar to take his turn to speak, but Zophar was silent. Perhaps Zophar felt it was a waste of time to argue with Job anymore.

In these three chapters, Job recalled the blessings of the past (Job 29), lamented the sufferings of the present (Job 30), and challenged God to vindicate him in the future (Job 31). He climaxed his speech with sixteen "if I have..." statements and put himself under oath, challenging God either to condemn him or vindicate him. It was as though Job were saying, "We've talked long enough! I really don't care what you three men think, because God is my Judge; and I rest my case with Him. Now, let Him settle the matter one way or another, once and for all."

1. Job looks back at life's joys (Job 29)
Job had opened his defense by saying that he wished he had never been born (Job 3). Now he closed his defense by re-

membering the blessings he and his family had enjoyed prior to his crisis. This is a good reminder that we should try to see life in a balanced way. Yes, God permits us to experience difficulties and sorrows, but God also sends victories and joys. "Shall we receive good at the hand of God, and shall we not receive evil?" (2:10) C.H. Spurgeon said that too many people write their blessings in the sand but engrave their sorrows in marble.

"Oh, that I were as in months past, as in the days when God preserved me!" (29:2) When we are experiencing trials, it's natural for us to long for "the good old days"; but our longing will not change our situation. Someone has defined "the good old days" as "a combination of a bad memory and a good imagination." In Job's case, however, his memory was accurate, and "the good old days" really were good.

There is a ministry in memory if we use it properly. Moses admonished Israel to remember the way God had led them and cared for them (Deut. 8:2). In fact, the word "remember" is found fourteen times in Deuteronomy and the word "forget" nine times. In days of disappointment, it's good to "remember the years of the right hand of the Most High" (Ps. 77:10-11; see 42:6). But the past must be a rudder to guide us and not an anchor to hold us back. If we try to duplicate today what we experienced yesterday, we may find ourselves in a rut that robs us of maturity.

It is significant that Job mentioned as his number-one joy *the presence of God in his home* (Job 29:2-6). God watched over him and shared His "intimate friendship" with him (v. 4, NIV). The light of God was upon Job, and God's presence was with him and his children. God was the source of all of Job's wealth and success, when his "path was drenched with cream and the rock poured out . . . streams of olive oil" (v. 6, NIV). (Zophar promised Job "honey and cream" if he would repent. See 20:17, and note Deut. 32:13-14; 33:24.)

There is one especially poignant note in this opening statement: Job wished he were back in the prime of life (Job 29:4). While this is a natural desire, it is also a dangerous one. *If we focus so much on the glories of the past that we ignore the opportunities of the present, we may end up unprepared to meet the future.* That future will come whether we like it or not. Few people eagerly anticipate old age and the special problems that it brings, but we can't avoid it. It's a proven fact that those who have the most birthdays live the longest, and those who live the longest become the oldest; and old people eventually die.

Remember the "never die" jokes? Old skiers never die: they just go downhill. Old bakers never die: they just fail to rise. Old football players never die: they just fumble away. Old golfers never die: they just lose their drive. We may think *we* will never die, but we will, unless the Lord returns to take us to heaven; and this means that we must prepare for old age and death. It is futile to look back with regret; it is faith to look ahead with rejoicing.

"To know how to grow old is the master work of wisdom," wrote Henri Amiel, "and one of the most difficult chapters in the great art of living."

Job next listed the joy of *respect from others* (vv. 7-11). When he walked through the city, the young men stepped aside to let him pass. He had his seat at the city gate with the leading men of the city, and even they ceased their speaking when he arrived. Wherever he went, he was treated with respect. "Whoever heard me spoke well of me, and those who saw me commended me" (v. 11, NIV).

His third source of joy was *ministry to others* (vv. 12-17). What God gave to him, Job shared with others. Eliphaz had accused Job of exploiting the poor and needy (22:5-9), but Job denied it. These verses describe the ministry of a compassionate man who brought help and happiness to many. Job strengthened righteousness and justice in the city (29:14; Isa. 59:17) as he helped the handicapped, provided for the needy, and even defended the strangers. But Job did not stop with assisting the needy; he also confronted the wicked and broke their power (Job 29:17). Job compared the wicked to fierce animals that were ready to devour the weak, but he came and snatched the victims from their very jaws.

Confidence in the future (vv. 18-20) was another source of joy to Job before his calamities came upon him. God was blessing Job, and Job was sharing those blessings with others; so he had every reason to believe that life would continue that way for many years. He was confident that he would stay fresh and vigorous, live to an old age, and die in peace and glory. He saw himself as a deeply rooted tree that would go on bearing fruit (v. 19; Ps. 92:12-14). Since children are sometimes pictured as arrows (127:3-5), Job 29:20 suggests that Job expected to maintain his physical vigor and beget many children.

His final source of joy was the *privilege of speaking words of encouragement and help* (vv. 21-25). He was indeed a Barnabas, "a son of encouragement" (Acts 4:36, NKJV), whose words were respected and appreciated. When he spoke, it was as gentle and refreshing as the rain. When he smiled, it lit up the whole situation and gave people hope. Job's approval was like the dawning of a new day! He was a leader who helped the perplexed make wise decisions and gave the mourners fresh comfort and hope.

Yes, Job had enjoyed a rich and rewarding life; but now all of that was gone.

2. Job looks around at God's judgment (Job 30)

From the delightful past, Job is suddenly thrust back into the dismal and disappointing present. You can almost hear him groan his first words, "But now" (Job 30:1; see vv. 9, 16). Job was wise enough to know that he had to face the reality of the present and not escape into the memory of the past. People who refuse to come to grips with life are in danger of losing touch with reality, and soon they lose touch with themselves.

"In their unsuccessful effort to fulfill their needs, no matter what behavior they choose," writes psychiatrist William Glasser, "all patients have a common characteristic: *They all deny the reality of the world around them*" (*Reality Therapy*, p. 6). By refusing to live in the past and by honestly facing reality, Job took a giant step in maturity and integrity. In his lament, Job contrasted his present situation with the past and showed how everything had been changed by the judgment of God. His five "complaints" parallel the joys that he named in chapter 29:

"I have no respect" (30:1-15, see 29:7-11)
"I have no blessing" (30:16-23, see 29:2-6)
"I have no help" (30:24-25, see 29:12-17)
"I have no future" (30:26-28, see 29:18-20)
"I have no ministry" (30:29-31, see 29:21-25)

"I have no respect" (Job 30:1-15). Young men who once stepped aside for Job (Job 29:8) now mocked him and even spit in his face (30:1, 9-10). But the worst part of this experience was that these young men were the sons of men so despicable that Job compared their fathers to donkeys wandering in the desert. He called them "children of fools, yea, children of base men" (v. 8). They were outcasts from society who had to forage in the wilderness to find food and fuel for their fires. At one time, Job had been the greatest man in the East; and now he was the song of the rabble (v. 9).

These men were unworthy to carry Job's sandals, and now they were openly ridiculing him. What made the difference?

Job was now an outcast like themselves. When Job's bow was "renewed in [his] hand"—a symbol of vigor and success (29:20)—these men respected him. But God had "loosed" his cord and afflicted him, so these rebels set aside their restraint and despised him (30:11). When formerly they had honored Job, it was not because they respected his character and integrity. It was because they respected his position and wealth and hoped to benefit from his favor. Their friendship was fickle, and their respect was hypocritical.

Because this rabble had "thrown off restraint" (v. 11, NIV), they made life miserable for Job. Job pictured them as a ruthless army, building siege ramps, laying traps for his feet, breaking down his defenses, and attacking him (vv. 12-14). They were also like a storm that frightened Job, blew away all his dignity, and destroyed his safety like the wind blows a passing cloud (v. 15).

Job experienced sufferings similar to those of our Lord Jesus Christ. The basest of people falsely accused Him (Matt. 26:59-64), spat upon Him (v. 67), and ridiculed Him while He was suffering (Luke 23:35-39); and He became "the song of the drunkards" (Ps. 69:12). Job didn't know it, but he was being honored by God to share in "the fellowship of His [Christ's] sufferings" (Phil. 3:10). Though sitting in an ash heap, Job had been promoted in the highest possible way!

"I have no blessing" (Job 30:16-23). "And now . . . the days of affliction have taken hold upon me," groaned Job (v. 16). What a contrast to the days of cream and oil! (29:6) Instead of enriching him with blessing, God was robbing him of even the basic enjoyments of life. In the daytime, Job endured unbearable suffering; and at night, God wrestled with him, made his clothing like a straitjacket, and threw him in the mud (30:16-19, NIV). Every night, God wrestled with Job; and Job lost.

Job prayed to God. He even stood up and cried out for

deliverance; but his prayers were unanswered (v. 20). Instead of God's hand bringing help, it only attacked Job ruthlessly and tossed him about like a feather in a storm (vv. 21-22). Job begged for his life, but death seemed inevitable (1:23).

"I have no help" (Job 30:24-25). Job had faithfully helped others in their need (29:12-17), but now nobody would help him. They wouldn't weep with him or even touch him. He was treated like a leper who might contaminate them, or like a condemned man whom God might destroy at any time. It just wasn't wise to get too close.

Where were the people that Job had helped? Surely some of them would have wanted to show their appreciation by encouraging their benefactor in his time of need. But nobody came to his aid. Mark Twain wrote, "If you pick up a starving dog and make him prosperous, he will not bite you. This is the principal difference between a dog and a man."

Our motive for serving others is certainly not to obligate them to serve us (Luke 14:12-14). We help others because we love Christ and want to glorify Him (Matt. 5:16), and because we sympathize with their needs and want to help them (Rom. 12:15; Luke 10:25-37). Missionary doctor Wilfred Grenfell said, "The service we render for others is really the rent we pay for our room on this earth."

"I have no future" (Job 30:26-28). During the days of his prosperity, Job had expected to enjoy a long and comfortable life and a peaceful death (29:18-20); but now that was all changed. He looked for good, but God sent evil; he looked for light, but God sent darkness. Instead of comfort and peace, he experienced constant turmoil within. "The churning inside me never stops; days of suffering confront me" (30:27, NIV).

The British essayist William Hazlitt wrote, "Hope is the best possession. None are completely wretched but those who are without hope, and few are reduced so low as that." Job was, and even the Lord seemed not to care. Job's body was weak and feverish, and his skin was black from disease.

"I have no ministry" (Job 30:29-31). In the past, Job's words had brought encouragement and hope to many (29:21-25); but now his words were like the howling of the jackals and the moaning of the owls and ostriches (Micah 1:8). Because his hope was dead, Job's song was a funeral dirge. His harp and flute were tuned to a minor key. How could he speak encouraging words to others when he himself was in the pit of discouragement? "And where is now my hope?" he had asked earlier in the debate. "As for my hope, who shall see it?" (Job 17:15)

3. Job looks ahead for God's justice (Job 31)

This chapter records Job's final defense. It is like a legal document in which Job puts himself under oath before God and asks for judgment to fall if God can prove him wrong (Job 31:35-37). Job's only hope was that God would hear his cry and vindicate his name. He could die in peace if he knew that his enemies had been silenced and his reputation restored. In sixteen "if I have . . ." statements, Job reviews his life and relationships and asks God to pass judgment. "I sign now my defense" (v. 35, NIV), said Job as he made the oath official and signed the document. "I rest my case!"

In verses 33-37, Job asked God ("my adversary"=judge) to give him three things: a hearing, an answer to his charges, and a document to prove his innocence. If God couldn't do these things, then Job was willing that God send the curses included in Job's oath. Job was prepared to give God an accounting of his every step if that's what it would take to bring the case to an end. Job had nothing to hide; he was not a hypocrite, cringing for fear of the people (vv. 33-34).

Job the man (Job 31:1-12). Job mentions three specific sins that could trip up any man: lust (vv. 1-4), deceit (vv. 5-8), and adultery (vv. 9-12).

117

(1) Lust is the first step toward sin, and sin is the first step toward death (James 1:13-16). It is one thing to see and admire an attractive person, but it is quite something else to look *for the purpose of lusting in the heart.* Jesus said, "Everyone who is looking at a woman in order to indulge his sexual passion for her, already committed adultery with her in his heart" (Matt. 5:28, WUEST). While sin in the heart is not as destructive as sin actually committed, it is the first step toward the act; and you never know where a polluted imagination will lead you. Furthermore, God above looks down and sees both our actions and "the thoughts and intents of the heart" (Heb. 4:12-13); and He will judge both. "Is it not ruin for the wicked, disaster for those who do wrong?" (Job 31:3, NIV)

(2) Deceit is the second sin that Job denies (vv. 5-8). He never used deception in his business dealings in order to make more money. In fact, he wouldn't even walk with those who did such things. His scales were honest (Lev. 19:35-37; Prov. 11:1), and he was not afraid for God to weigh him! (Dan. 5:27) His heart had not been covetous nor were his hands defiled because he had not taken what was not his. If he were guilty of covetousness and deception, then Job was willing for his next season's crops to be taken by others.

(3) Adultery (Job 31:9-12) begins with lust in the heart (v. 1) that leads to furtive attempts to satisfy sinful desires. Job had never lurked about to see when his neighbor's wife would be alone. If he was guilty, then he was willing for his own wife to become another man's slave and mistress! Adultery is a heinous crime that brings shameful and painful consequences in this life, and judgment in the next (Prov. 6:27-29; Eph. 5:3-7; Heb. 13:4).

Job the employer (Job 31:13-15). So careful was Job in his self-examination that he even included his treatment of his servants. Most masters in that day would have ignored this aspect of life. Job treated his servants generously and settled their grievances fairly because he knew that one day he would have to give an account to God (v. 14; Eph. 6:9). He also knew that he was created by the same God who created them and that he was born in the same way.

Job the neighbor (Job 31:16-23, 29-32). In reply to the false accusations of Eliphaz (22:6-9), Job had already told how he had cared for the poor and needy (29:12-17); but now he repeated it as a part of his oath. He was not boasting; he was defending himself before men and seeking vindication from God. If he had lifted his hand in court against any man, Job hoped that God would rip that arm from its socket.

Job was concerned for the needs of widows, orphans, and the poor. He provided them with food and clothing and came to their defense in court. He even treated them like members of his own family and cared for them until they could care for themselves. God had given Job his wealth, and God could take it away from him if he didn't share it with others (31:23). But Job was also a good neighbor to his enemies (vv. 29-31) and to strangers passing through town (v. 32). Because Job was a wealthy and powerful sheik, no doubt there were many people who envied him and hated him; yet Job was kind to them. He didn't gloat over their misfortunes (Ex. 23:4-5; Prov. 24:17-18; Matt. 5:43-47) or ask God to curse them (Rom. 12:17-21).

Job was also generous to strangers, giving them food to eat and a place to spend the night. None of Job's servants could ever accuse their master of being selfish (Job 31:31, NIV). His home was open to all, and he was generous with his gifts.

Job the worshiper (Job 31:24-28). Job worshiped God with a sincere heart. He didn't worship his wealth or trust it for his security, nor did he take credit for earning it (Deut. 8:17-18). Eliphaz had accused Job of making gold his god (Job 22:24-25), but Job denied it. He did not worship gold nor did he worship the heavenly bodies and secretly "throw them a kiss of homage" (1 Kings 19:18, NIV). If Job committed such a sin, men might not see it; but God would see it and would judge Job for being unfaithful to Him.

Job the steward (Job 31:38-40). In verses 35-37, Job had completed his "official demand" for a hearing and signed the document. Then he remembered one more area that needed to be covered: his stewardship of the land God had given him. Job treated the land as though it were a person. If he had abused the land, it would have cried out against him and wept in pain (v. 38). If Job's field hands had been overworked and underpaid, then God would have had every reason to give Job a harvest of weeds instead of wheat and barley.

Review Job's oath and you will discover that he has asked God to send some terrible judgments if he is guilty of any of these sins: others will eat his harvest and uproot his crops (v. 8); his wife will become another man's servant and mistress (v. 10); his arm will fall from his shoulder (v. 22); his harvest will be weeds and thistles (v. 40). He made it clear that he was willing to face the righteous judgment of God (vv. 14, 23, 28) along with these other judgments.

When the words of Job were ended, everybody sat in silence, wondering what would happen next. Would God send immediate judgment and prove Job guilty? Or would He accept Job's challenge, appear to him, and give Job opportunity to defend himself? Perhaps God would speak from heaven and answer Job's questions.

Job had challenged God because he was sure God would vindicate him. Job's three friends were sure that God would condemn him.

What will God do? The answer may surprise you!

*"A vain man may become proud and imagine himself pleasing to
all when he is in reality a universal nuisance."*
Benedict Spinoza

Elihu Has the Answers

Job was silent. He had ended his defense and given oath that
he was not guilty of the sins he had been accused of by his
friends. Job had challenged God either to vindicate him or
pass sentence on him. The trial had gone on long enough,
and it was time for the Judge to act.

Job's three friends were silent, appalled that Job had dared
to speak so boldly *to* God and *about* God. They were sure that
God's judgment of Job was the next thing on the agenda.

God was silent. No fire came from heaven, and no voice
spoke in divine wrath. The silence was God's eloquent witness to the three friends that they were wrong in what they
had said both about Job and about God. It was also God's
witness to Job that the God of the universe is not at the beck
and call of His creatures. God doesn't appear just because
somebody thinks it's time for a showdown.

At the famous "Speaker's Corner" in London's Hyde Park,
a man denouncing Christianity issued this challenge: "If
there is a God, I will give Him five minutes to strike me
dead!" He took out his watch and waited. After five minutes,
he smiled and said, "My friends, this proves that there is no
God!"

A Christian believer in the crowd called to him, "Do you think you can exhaust the patience of Almighty God in five minutes?"

However, in the crowd around the ash heap, one person was not silent. It was Elihu, a man so unknown that his full pedigree had to be given so people could identify him (Job 32:2). Neither Job (1:1) nor his three friends (2:11) needed that kind of detailed identification for others to know them.

Elihu gave a long speech—six chapters in our Bible—in which he explained the character of God and applied this truth to Job's situation. One way to outline his speech is as follows:

1. God is speaking through me (Job 32; note v. 8)
2. God is gracious (Job 33; note v. 24)
3. God is just (Job 34–35; note 34:10-12)
4. God is great (Job 36–37; note 36:5, 26)

While Elihu said some of the same things as the other speakers, his purpose was different from theirs. He was not trying to prove that Job was a sinner, but that Job's view of God was wrong. Elihu introduced a new truth into the debate: that God sends suffering, not necessarily to punish us for our sins, but to keep us from sinning (33:18, 24) and to make us better persons (36:1-15). Paul would have agreed with the first point (2 Cor. 12:7-10) and the writer of Hebrews with the second (Heb. 12:1-11).

Let's consider the first two of Elihu's affirmations about God.

1. God is speaking through me (Job 32)
Elihu emphasized that he had waited patiently before speaking, and he gave two reasons. For one thing, he was younger than Job and the three friends; and youth must respect age

and experience (Job 32:4, 6-7). It would have been a terrible breach of etiquette had Elihu interrupted his elders.

His second reason was because he wanted to hear the complete debate and have all the arguments before him (v. 11; Prov. 18:13). The fact that Elihu quoted from their speeches indicates that he had listened closely and remembered what each man said (Job 32:12). Like many "young theologians," Elihu had a bit of youthful conceit in his speeches ("Hear what I know!"—vv. 6, 10, 17; 33:1-3); but for the most part, he was a sincere young man who really thought he could help Job find answers to his questions.

Having introduced himself into the discussion, Elihu then gave four reasons to explain why it was important for him to speak and for them to listen. After all, he was a "nobody"; and he had to convince them that what he had to say was worth hearing.

He was indignant (Job 32:1-3, 5). Four times in these verses we are told that Elihu was angry. He was angry at the three friends for not refuting Job, and he was angry at Job for justifying himself rather than God. Job claimed that God was wrong, and the three friends couldn't prove that Job was wrong! Bildad, Zophar, and Eliphaz had given up the cause (v. 15) and were waiting for God to come and deal personally with Job (vv. 12-13). Elihu was disgusted at their failure.

"It is easy to fly into a passion—anybody can do that," wrote Aristotle. "But to be angry with the right person to the right extent and at the right time and with the right object and in the right way—that is not easy, and it is not everyone who can do it."

He was inspired (Job 32:8-10). Age should bring wisdom, but there is no guarantee that it will (Prov. 16:31). Alas, there are old fools as well as young fools! As a younger man, Elihu couldn't claim to have wide experience in the ways of God and men; but he claimed to have something better: the insight of the Spirit of God. The Holy Spirit had instructed Elihu's spirit (1 Cor. 2:11) and revealed God's truths to him. Elihu didn't need the wisdom that comes with experience, for he had been taught by God (Ps. 119:97-100).

This explains why Elihu repeatedly exhorted Job and his friends to listen to him (Job 32:10; 33:1, 31, 33; 34:2, 10, 16; 37:14). It also explains why he emphasized the phrases "mine opinion" (32:6, 10, 17; "what I know" in the NIV) and "my words" (33:1-3). It isn't every day that you can hear a man who has been inspired by God, so you had better listen!

He was impartial (Job 32:14, 21-22). "Now he has not directed his words against me, so I will not answer him with your words" (v. 14, NKJV). Elihu made it clear that he had no reason for taking sides since neither Job nor any of the three friends had attacked him personally. Elihu also said that he would avoid rehashing the same arguments that they had used, though he didn't fully live up to that promise.

Elihu may have been impartial but he was by no means neutral. He was too angry for that! He promised to deal only with issues, but some of the things he said in his anger were more personal than philosophical. But he did keep his promise and not flatter anyone (vv. 21-22). As you read his speech, you will notice that six times he addressed Job by his first name (33:1; 34:5, 7, 35, 36; 35:16), something that even Job's three closest friends had not done in their many speeches. In the East, it was most unusual for a younger man to address his elders in such a familiar way.

He was impelled (Job 32:16-20). Elihu had waited a long time for the opportunity to speak; and while he was waiting, the pressure within him had built up to the bursting point. He was full of words like a wineskin full of wine. As the new wine ferments, it produces gas that inflates the wineskin; and if the skin is old and dry, it will break (Matt. 9:17). If anybody had suggested that Elihu was "full of gas," he would have been offended; because to him, it was God's Spirit compelling him to speak. Elihu had a mandate from God to tell everybody what he knew. Little did he know that, when God finally appeared on the scene, He would completely ignore Elihu and all that he said.

2. God is gracious (Job 33)

This is a remarkable speech because it introduces into the debate a new insight into the purpose of suffering. Job's friends had argued that his suffering was evidence that God was punishing him for his sins, but Elihu now argues that sometimes God permits us to suffer *to keep us from sin.* In other words, suffering may be *preventive* and not *punitive.* (See Paul's experience recorded in 2 Cor. 12:7-10.) God does all He can to keep us from sinning and going into the pit of death, and this is evidence of His grace (Job 33:24).

Before launching into his argument, Elihu assured Job that his words were sincere and given by God's Spirit, so Job had no reason to be afraid (vv. 1-7). Elihu didn't claim to have any "inside track" with God; he was made of clay just like Job. He promised not to be heavy-handed in his speaking, and he invited Job to feel free to reply. Elihu didn't want this to be a monologue, but that's exactly what it turned out to be. Either Job was silenced by what Elihu said, or Elihu didn't pause long enough for Job to speak (see vv. 31, 33), or Job didn't think it was worthwhile to respond.

Having assured Job that his words would be helpful and not hurtful, Elihu then proceeded to quote what Job had said about himself (vv. 8-11). Job's words will form the premise for Elihu's argument.

First, Elihu said that Job had claimed to be sinless (v. 9), *which was not what Job had said.* That Job claimed to be sinless was Zophar's interpretation, not Job's declaration

(11:4). Job did say that he did not lie (6:30), that he was not wicked (10:7), that he was just and upright (12:4), and that he had not disobeyed God (23:11-12); but he never said he was sinless. He consistently maintained his integrity (2:3; 27:4-5), but never said he was perfect. In fact, he denied perfection (9:20-21). Elihu's basic premise was weak because he confused Zophar's words with Job's words. It may have sounded like Job was claiming to be *sinless,* but he was only saying that he was *blameless,* which is an entirely different thing.

Second, Elihu quoted Job as saying that God was unjust and was treating him like an enemy (33:10-11). This quotation was true (13:24, 27; 16:9; 19:7, 11). In his speeches, Job had repeatedly asked God why He was attacking him and why He didn't give him a fair trial. Elihu's great concern was not to debate what Job said about himself but to refute what Job said about God.

This "young theologian" knew something about public speaking because Job 33 is a model address. First, he stated his thesis in verses 12-14: God is greater than man and speaks to him in ways that he may not always recognize. He then described three different ways that God may speak to man: dreams and visions (vv. 15-18), suffering (vv. 19-22), and the ministry of the mediating angel (vv. 23-33).

The word "pit" is used five times in verses 14-33. God's purpose in discipline is to save people from death (James 5:19-20) by breaking their pride and bringing them back to the place of obedience (Job 33:17-18). God seeks to keep them from the pit (v. 18), but rebellious sinners *draw near* to the pit (v. 22), then *go down* to the pit (v. 24), and *into* the pit (v. 28). When it is almost too late, the Mediator brings them *back from* the pit (v. 30), and they are rescued. "God does all these things to a man—twice, even three times—to turn back his soul from the pit, that the light of life may shine on him" (vv. 29-30, NIV). God is "not willing that any should perish" (2 Peter 3:9).

126

Dreams and visions (Job 33:15-18). In Bible times, God sometimes spoke to people through dreams and visions; today His Spirit directs us primarily through His Word (Heb. 1:1-2). If sinners have frightening visions or dreams, it might shock them and keep them from committing the sins they had planned. Job himself experienced terrifying dreams (Job 7:13-14), and Eliphaz had an unforgettable night vision (4:12-21). God sends dreams and visions in order to "open the ears of men," which gets them to listen to God's Word and obey. If they don't humble themselves, they may go down to the pit of death.

A man stopped a stranger on a New York City street and said, "Can you share a dream with me? I'm on my way to my psychiatrist, and I haven't slept for a week. I desperately need a dream to tell him!"

Not all dreams have hidden meanings, and not all dreams come from God with special messages in them. More than one nightmare has been caused by improper diet! People who plan their lives around what they learn from the "dream book" are asking for confusion rather than direction. God can use dreams to shake the confidence of a proud sinner, but this is not His normal approach today.

Suffering (Job 33:19-22). In *The Problem of Pain,* C.S. Lewis says, "God whispers to us in our pleasures, speaks in our conscience, but shouts in our pains: it is His megaphone to rouse a deaf world." God sometimes uses pain to warn us, humble us, and bring us to the place of submission (Heb. 12:1-11). Elihu describes a sick man, suffering on his bed, wasting away because he has no appetite. (Is this a picture of Job? See 6:7; 7:3-6; 16:8; 17:7; 19:20.) But this man is suffering because God wants to get his attention and prevent him from breaking God's law.

It is a mistake to say that all suffering comes from God, because we cause some suffering ourselves. Careless driving may lead to an accident that will make many people suffer. Improper eating may upset the body and cause abused organs to protest with pain. There is pleasure in sin (Heb. 11:25), but sin causes suffering. "The way of transgressors is hard" (Prov. 13:15). If people defy the Law of God, there is a price to pay.

And we must not say that all suffering is a punishment for sin. Elihu argues that sometimes God permits suffering *in order to keep people from sinning and going to the pit.* God gave Paul a "thorn in the flesh" to keep him from getting proud, and Paul learned to thank God for it (2 Cor. 12:7-10). Elihu hoped that Job would submit to God, accept his painful situation, and get from it the blessings God had for him.

Nobody wants to be sick; everybody prays for healing. But the British Congregational theologian P.T. Forsyth said, "It is a greater thing to pray for pain's conversion than its removal." That's what Paul learned to do with his thorn in the flesh. What might have been a weapon to tear him down became, by the grace of God, a tool to build him up! Had he lost that messenger of pain, Paul might have become proud of his spiritual achievements; and that pride might have led him into sin.

Elihu has presented two ways that God speaks to people in order to keep them from the pit: visions and dreams, and sickness and pain. Now he presents the third.

The ministry of the mediating angel (Job 33:23-33). The Book of Job opens with a description of God's heavenly court where the angels ("sons of God") report for duty (Job 33; 1:6ff; 2:1ff). Eliphaz mentions the angels in 4:18 and possibly in 5:1 ("holy ones"), and angels are also mentioned in 38:7 as rejoicing at the creation of the world. Except for this present passage, these are the only references to angels in the book.

Elihu paints an awesome picture. The sinner has been warned by dreams and visions and has been chastened by sickness and suffering. He is drawing near to the grave, and "the destroyers" ("messengers of death," NIV) are about to capture him (33:22). Then a special messenger suddenly stands up ("one among a thousand") and pleads his case. This messenger has a twofold ministry: he tells the sufferer what he ought to do (v. 23), and he intercedes with God to have the person restored.

It seems likely that this interceding angel is the Angel of the Lord, our Lord Jesus Christ, the Mediator who gave His life as a ransom for sinners (1 Tim. 2:5; Mark 10:45). As the Angel of the Lord, the Son of God visited the earth in Old Testament times to deliver special messages and accomplish important tasks (Gen. 16:9; 22:11; Ex. 3:2; Jud. 6:11). But Elihu saw this Angel not only as a Mediator between God and men, but also as the Provider of the ransom for sinners.

This is the heavenly "mediator" that Job has been asking for throughout the debate! Job wanted an "umpire" to bring him and God together for a trial (Job 9:33), a heavenly "witness" to argue his case before God (16:19), a "redeemer" who would vindicate him even after his death (19:25). The ministry of this Angel is purely an act of God's grace (33:24). "Spare him from going down to the pit; I have found a ransom for him" (v. 24, NIV). That sounds like our Lord Jesus Christ, who is both our Mediator and our Ransom (1 Tim. 2:5-6).

The concept of "the ransom" is woven into the fabric of biblical theology. The Hebrew word means "to atone for sin by the offering of a substitute." The condemned sinner can't be set free by the paying of some cheap price such as money (Ps. 49:7-9), good works, or good intentions. It must be a ransom that God will accept, and God asks for the shedding of blood (Lev. 16–17). Job didn't ask his three friends to ransom him because he knew they couldn't (Job 6:21-23). Only God can provide the ransom, and He did. If God has provided a ransom for lost sinners about to go down into the pit, *how foolish of them not to receive it!*

Elihu promised Job that God would radically alter his situation if only he would humble himself. It would be like a "new birth"! (33:25; see John 3) He would once more enjoy prayer and fellowship with God (Job 33:26). He would confess his sins and admit that God had punished him far less than he deserved (v. 27). Job would move out of the darkness into the light and gladly bear witness of God's redemption (v. 28).

Job 33:31-33 suggests that Elihu wanted Job's response, but at the same time Elihu wanted Job to keep quiet! Elihu was filled to the brim with his subject and didn't want to stop talking. But Job didn't reply *because he was waiting for God to speak.* Job had already stated his case and thrown down the gauntlet. What Elihu thought about him or said to him made little difference to Job.

Job had taken his case to a much higher court; and when Elihu finishes speaking, the Judge will appear.

"What, then, is the God I worship?. . . You are the most hidden from us and yet the most present among us, the most beautiful and yet the most strong, ever enduring; and yet we cannot comprehend you."

St. Augustine

Elihu Explains and Defends God

Theology ("the science of God") used to be called "the queen of sciences" because it deals with the most important knowledge we can have, the knowledge of God. Theology is a necessary science, but it is also a difficult science; for it is our attempt to know the Unknowable (Rom. 11:33-36). God has revealed Himself in creation, in providence, in His Word, and supremely in His Son; but our understanding of what God has revealed may not always be clear.

"The essence of idolatry," wrote A.W. Tozer, "is the entertainment of thoughts about God that are unworthy of Him" *(The Knowledge of the Holy,* Harper & Row, p. 11). So, whoever attempts to explain and defend the Almighty must have the humble heart of a worshiper; for "knowledge puffs up, but love builds up" (1 Cor. 8:1, NIV).

As you read Elihu's speeches, you get the impression that he was not growing; he was swelling. You also get the impression that his listeners' minds were wandering, because he kept exhorting them to listen carefully (Job 33:1, 31, 33; 34:2, 10, 16). In the last two thirds of his speech, Elihu explained and defended *the justice of God* (Job 34–35) and *the greatness of God* (Job 36–37).

1. God is just (Job 34–35)

Elihu had promised not to use flattery (Job 32:21), but he came close to it in 34:2 when he addressed his audience as "wise men" and "men of learning" (NIV). Actually, he was flattering himself; because if these "learned wise men" were willing to listen to him, they must have thought that he was more learned and wise than they! Quoting Job's words (v. 3; 12:11), Elihu urged them to use discernment as they "tasted" his words, so that he and they might "learn together what is good" (34:4, NIV). Elihu compared his speaking to the enjoyment of a tasteful and nourishing meal.

Elihu listed two of Job's complaints to be discussed: "God is unjust" (vv. 5-6) and "There is no profit in serving God" (vv. 7-9). He answered the first complaint in verses 10-37 and the second in Job 35.

"God is unjust" (Job 34:5-6, 10-37). The injustice of God was one of the major themes in Job's speeches. He felt that he was being treated like a sinner, and yet God would not "come to court" and tell Job what he had done wrong. (See 9:2, 17-20; 19:6-7; 27:2.) Elihu recalled Job saying that he was innocent and had been denied justice (34:5; 10:7; 6:29), and that God was shooting arrows at him (34:6; 6:4).

Elihu presented three arguments to prove that there is no injustice with God. To begin with, *if God is unjust, then He is not God* (34:10-15). "Far be it from God, that He should do wickedness, and from the Almighty, that He should commit iniquity" (v. 10). "It is unthinkable that God would do wrong, that the Almighty would pervert justice" (v. 12, NIV). Abraham asked, "Shall not the Judge of all the earth do right?" (Gen. 18:25) and the obvious answer is yes!

If God is truly God, then He is perfect; and if He is perfect, then He cannot do wrong. An unjust God would be as unthinkable as a square circle or a round triangle. According to Elihu, what seems injustice to us is really justice: God is paying sinners back for what they do (Job 34:11). In fact, God is so just that He has ordained that *sin itself will punish the evildoer.* (See Pss. 7:15; 9:15-16; 35:8.) There is no way to escape the justice of God.

Elihu emphasized that God is sovereign, and a sovereign God can be indicted by no law or judged by no court. The king can do no wrong. God was not *appointed* to His throne, so He can't be taken from it (Job 34:13). To say that God is unjust is to say that He is not God and therefore has no right to be on the throne. But God controls our very breath and can take our lives away in an instant (vv. 14-15; Acts 17:25, 28). "It is because of the Lord's mercies that we are not consumed, because His compassions fail not" (Lam. 3:22).

The Book of Job magnifies the sovereignty of God. From the very first chapter, it is obvious that God is in control; for even Satan is told what he can and cannot do. During the debate, it appears that God is absent; but He is aware of how Job feels and what Job and his friends say. Thirty-one times in the Book of Job, God is called "the Almighty." Elihu was right on target: God is sovereign and cannot do wrong.

His second argument is that *if God were unjust, there could be no just government on earth* (Job 34:16-20). As a respected elder, Job had participated in local government and had helped to bring justice to the afflicted (29:7-17). But all human government was established by God (Gen. 9:1-7; Rom. 13:1-7); so if mortal man can execute justice on earth, why can't a holy and sovereign God execute justice from heaven? He can dethrone kings and remove nobles, and He shows no partiality (Dan. 4:25, 32, 35). If the God who rules the world were unjust, there could be no order or harmony; and everything would fall apart.

However, Elihu made a big mistake in singling out and emphasizing only one divine attribute, the justice of God; for God is also loving and gracious. (Bildad had made the same mistake in his speeches.) In His wisdom, God devised a plan of redemption that satisfies both His justice and His love (Rom. 3:21-31). Because of the Cross, God can redeem sinners and still magnify His righteousness and uphold His holy law.

Elihu's third argument is that *if God were unjust, then He must not see what is going on in the world* (Job 34:21-30). But God is omniscient and sees all things! A human judge, with his limitations, hears a case and makes the best decision he can, and sometimes he's wrong. But God sees every step we take, and there is no place where we can hide from Him (Ps. 139:7-12). Job wanted God to meet him in court so he could present his case, but what could Job tell God that God didn't already know? "God has no need to examine men further, that they should come before Him for judgment" (Job 34:23, NIV). Unlike human officials, God is not obligated to conduct an inquiry and gather evidence; He knows everything and can judge with perfect wisdom.

One of Job's complaints was that God was silent and had hidden His face from him (9:11; 23:1-9), but Elihu had an answer for that: "But if He remains silent, who can condemn Him? If He hides His face, who can see Him?" (34:29, NIV) In Job 24, Job had accused God of ignoring men's sins; but what right had he to judge the Judge? God waited 4 centuries before judging the wicked nations in Canaan (Gen. 15:13-16) and 120 years before sending the Flood (6:3). Sinners should be grateful that God gives them time to repent (2 Peter 3:9).

God rules over nations and individuals (Job 34:29), but He is not responsible for their sins; for He gives them freedom to make decisions. They also have the freedom to turn from their sins and trust God. Because of this, Elihu closes this part of his speech with an appeal to Job that he confess his sins and repent (vv. 31-33). "Ask God to teach you what you don't know," he counsels, "and promise not to sin like this again" (see v. 32). God rewards us on *His* terms, not our terms; and one of His requirements is that we repent and turn from our sins.

Elihu paused and gave Job opportunity to speak (v. 33), but Job said nothing. This may have angered Elihu even more because he ended this part of the address with a terrible accusation against Job. He said that Job lacked knowledge and insight, that he was rebellious and spoke proudly against God. Clapping the hands is today a sign of approval, but in that day it was a gesture of mockery and contempt (27:23; Lam. 2:15). Elihu concluded that Job needed *even more testing!* (Job 34:36) Perhaps that would bring him to his senses.

Having disposed of Job's first complaint, Elihu turns to the second one.

"There is no profit in obeying God" (Job 34:7-9; 35:1-16). Again, Elihu tries to throw Job's own words back in his face: "I am innocent" (10:7; 12:4; 27:6) and, "What have I gained by obeying God?" (9:29-31; 21:15) Job did make the first statement, but the second is not an accurate quotation of his words. *Job never did bargain with God as Satan said he would (1:9, 21; 2:9-10).* Eliphaz had discussed this topic (Job 22) and had come to the conclusion that neither man's piety nor his iniquity could make any difference to the character of God. But Elihu felt it was important to deal with the theme again.

Elihu asked his listeners to look up to the heavens and see how far away the clouds were, and then imagine how far God's throne was from the earth (35:5-7). Can a man's sins or good deeds on earth exert such power that they will travel all that distance and change the Almighty in heaven?

Then Elihu asked them to consider human society (vv. 8-16). Our sins or good works may affect people around us (v. 8), but God is not affected by them. Certainly God grieves over man's sins (Gen. 6:6) and delights in the obedience of the faithful (Ps. 37:23); but our good deeds can't bribe Him, and our misdeeds can't threaten Him. God's character is the same whether men obey Him or disobey Him. God can't change for the better because He is perfect, and He can't change for the worse because He is holy.

God cares for the birds and beasts, and they trust Him (Job 35:11; Matt. 6:25-34); but men made in the image of God don't cry out to God until they are under a terrible burden of oppression (Job 35:9). They forget God until trouble comes. But God knows that their prayers are insincere, so He doesn't answer them (vv. 12-13). This explains why Job's prayers haven't been answered: his heart was not right with God (v. 14).

But even if God doesn't relieve the burden, He can give the trusting sufferer "songs in the night" (v. 10; Ps. 42:8; 77:6). "Any man can sing in the day," said Charles Spurgeon. "It is easy to sing when we can read the notes by daylight; but he is the skillful singer who can sing when there is not a ray of light by which to read." The Lord gave "songs in the night" to Jesus before He went to the cross (Matt. 26:30) and to Paul and Silas in the prison in Philippi (Acts 16:25). If God doesn't see fit to remove our burdens, He always gives strength to bear them—and a song to sing while doing it!

Elihu dismisses Job's complaint that he can't see God. The important thing is that *God sees Job* and knows his case completely (Job 35:14). Job's situation won't be changed by his empty talk and many words (v. 16), so the only thing for Job to do is wait and trust (v. 14).

God is gracious (Job 33), and God is just (Job 34–35); but God is also great and mighty (Job 36–37), and Elihu thought that Job needed to recognize how great God is.

2. God is great (Job 36–37)
"Behold, God is mighty" (Job 36:5). "Behold, God exalteth by His power" (v. 22). "Behold, God is great" (v. 26). In these

two chapters, Elihu magnifies the greatness of God in His *merciful purpose for man* (vv. 1-25) and in His *mighty power in nature* (36:26–37:13). He concludes his speech by making one last appeal to Job to fear the Lord and repent (vv. 14-24).

God's merciful purpose for man (Job 36:1-25). Elihu's self-importance reaches new heights as he introduces the last third of his speech (vv. 1-4). His listeners must have been getting restless; otherwise, why did he have to say, "Bear with me a little [longer]"? (v. 2) The statement "I will fetch my knowledge from afar" (v. 3) suggests that either he is boasting of wide knowledge or of getting his knowledge right from heaven. And to call himself "one perfect in knowledge" (v. 4, NIV) is hardly an evidence of humility!

(1) Explanation (vv. 5-15). The fact that God is great and mighty does not mean that He ignores man or has no concern for individuals. "God is mighty, but does not despise men; He is mighty and firm in His purpose" (v. 5, NIV). What is that purpose? To punish the wicked and help the afflicted ("poor," vv. 6, 15, KJV). Elihu contrasts God's dealings with the arrogant wicked and the afflicted righteous. "He does not keep the wicked alive, but gives justice to the afflicted" (v. 6, NASB).

Job thought that God was ignoring him, but God keeps His eyes on the righteous (v. 7; 1 Peter 3:12) and eventually transforms their circumstances. He lifts them from the ash heap to the throne (Luke 1:52-53) and sets them free from their chains (Job 36:7-8). He chastens us that He might correct us and teach us the right way to live. If we learn our lesson and obey, He will bless us once again. But if we rebel, He will destroy us (vv. 9-12).

The response of the heart is the key. The hypocrites ("godless in heart," NIV) only heap up wrath as they harden themselves against God. No matter how much God disciplines them, they refuse to cry out for help. But the humble in heart get God's message ("He speaks to them in their affliction," v. 15, NIV) and turn from their sins. The phrase "the unclean" in verse 14 refers to the male prostitutes at the various idolatrous shrines (Deut. 23:17). Elihu chose this image as a picture of the very depths of shame and sin. The wicked not only die young (Job 36:14; 20:5, 11), but they die in disgrace.

(2) Application (vv. 16-25). Job must make a decision. "He [God] is wooing you from the jaws of distress to a spacious place" (v. 16, NIV; Ps. 18:19). Job's table was laden with suffering when it could be laden with the choicest of foods. How would Job respond?

Elihu saw several dangers ahead for Job and tried to warn him. The first was that Job might look for some "shortcut" for getting out of trouble and thereby miss the message God had for him. Job might agree to let somebody "buy his way out," but no amount of money could do that (Job 36:18-19). *The Wall Street Journal* said it best: "Money is an article which may be used as a universal passport to everywhere except heaven, and as a universal provider for everything except happiness."

The second danger was that Job might consider taking his own life (v. 20). "The night" and "darkness" are images of death, and Job often expressed a longing to die (3:1-9, 20-23; 7:21; 10:18-22). Many sufferers have committed suicide in order to escape their hopeless situations, but there was not much danger that Job would take this route. Job was a man of faith and was not about to go into God's presence uninvited.

Elihu saw a third danger, that Job might give up all hope and turn to a life of sin (36:21). In my own pastoral ministry, I have counseled people who were so bitter against God that they abandoned their professions of faith and went back into the world. "If life is going to be this tough," they say, "then we might just as well enjoy ourselves while we can." They forget that there can be no true enjoyment without God, and that sin eventually brings its own harvest of suffering and sorrow.

Finally, Elihu urged Job to catch a new vision of the greatness of God and start praising Him (vv. 22-25). God wants to teach us through our sufferings (v. 22), and one evidence that we are learning our lessons is that we praise and thank Him, even for trials. "Glorify Him for His mighty works for which He is so famous" (v. 24, TLB). "Praise changes things" just as much as "prayer changes things."

God's mighty power in nature (Job 36:26–37:24). "Behold, God is great, and we know Him not" (36:26). This is the theme of the last part of Elihu's speech; and he illustrated it with the works of God in nature, specifically, God's control of His world during the seasons of the year.

(1) Autumn (36:27–37:5). In the East, after the heat and drought of summer, both the land and the people welcome the autumn rains. It is interesting to discover Elihu's insight into the "water cycle" of nature (evaporation, condensation, precipitation) and the need for electricity (lightning) to help the "system" work.

With the mind of a scientist but the heart of a poet, Elihu describes the storm. He begins with the formation of the clouds (36:26-29), then the release of power by the lightning (vv. 30-32), and then the sound of the thunder (36:33–37:5). To Elihu, the lightning is the weapon of God (36:32), and the thunder is the voice of God (37:2, 4-5). In the East, you can see a storm brewing miles away and with fascination watch as it approaches.

What was Elihu's response to the drama of the storm? For one thing, the storm reminded him of God's sovereignty and God's goodness. "This is the way He governs the nations and provides food in abundance" (36:31, NIV). It also aroused in him a sense of awe at the mighty power of God (37:1). David recorded a similar experience in Psalm 29.

(2) Winter (vv. 6-10). At some point, the autumn rains become winter ice and snow. Workers must stop their labor, and wild animals retreat to the protection of their dens. God breathes on the waters, and they freeze. What the weatherman calls "meteorological phenomena," Elihu calls the miracle work of Almighty God. Isaac Watts agreed with Elihu when he wrote:

> I sing the goodness of the Lord
> That filled the earth with food;
> He formed the creatures with His word,
> And then pronounced them good.
>
> There's not a plant or flower below
> But makes Thy glories known;
> And clouds arise and tempests blow
> By order from Thy throne.

(3) Spring (vv. 11-13). Eventually the warmer winds start to blow, the snow and ice melt, and the rain clouds appear once again. Elihu knew that the wind plays a most important part in the world's weather. Nobody can predict exactly what the wind will do (John 3:8), but God is in complete control (Ps. 148:8). The "water cycle" operates effectively: the clouds are full of water, the lightning flashes, and the rain falls. Sometimes God sends the storms for discipline (Job 37:13; Gen. 6–8; Ex. 9:13-26; 1 Sam. 12:16-19); but for the most part, the rain is the gift of His love and mercy (Job 37:13).

(4) Summer (vv. 14-18). Now the clouds "hang poised" (v. 16, NIV), and everything is still. The summer sun heats the air, the south wind (the "sirocco") blows from the desert, and people start to "swelter in [their] clothes" (v. 17, NIV). The

sky is like a brass mirror, and nobody feels like doing anything but resting.

But Eliphaz was doing much more than delivering a poetical, scientific lecture on the four seasons. He wanted Job to consider the greatness of God and the wonders of nature *and realize how little Job really knew about God and His working in this world.* Elihu asked Job three rhetorical questions—about the clouds, the lightning, the wind, and the rainless skies. "Can you explain these things?" he asked. "Can you control them?"

This led to Elihu's final thrust: "If you can't explain to us the everyday things of nature, then how will you ever prepare a court case to defend yourself before God?" He then warned Job that to challenge God might lead to Job's being swallowed up by God's judgment (v. 20). Verses 21-22 describe the "clear shining after rain" (2 Sam. 23:4), the blue sky, the bright sun, the "golden splendor" and "awesome majesty" of God (NIV). "You can't even look at the sun," says Elihu, "and yet you want to meet God face to face!"

Elihu's closing words remind us that, even though we can't fully understand God, we know that He is great and just and does not afflict men to no purpose. What should our personal response be? "Therefore, fear Him!" Job had come to that same conclusion after pondering the works of God in the world (Job 28:24-28).

It is possible that while Elihu was speaking, an actual storm was in the making in the distance; and when he finished, the storm broke—*and God was in the storm!*

Job will now get what he'd been asking for: a personal meeting with God. Was he ready? *Are we ready?*

INTERLUDE

With all his verbosity and lack of humility, Elihu did say some good things that Job needed to hear. Elihu's use of rhetorical questions in Job 37:14-18 prepared Job for the series of questions Jehovah would ask him in Job 38–41. Unlike the three friends, Elihu assessed Job's problem accurately: Job's *actions* may have been right—he was not the sinner his three friends described him to be—but his *attitudes* were wrong. He was not the "saint" Job saw himself to be. Job was slowly moving toward a defiant, self-righteous attitude that was not at all healthy. It was this "know-it-all" attitude that God exposed and destroyed when He appeared to Job and questioned him.

So, even though God said nothing about Elihu, the man did have a helpful ministry to Job. Unfortunately, Job wouldn't accept it.

"I had a million questions to ask God; but when I met Him, they all fled my mind; and it didn't seem to matter."
Christopher Morley

The Final Examination

The storm that Elihu had been describing finally broke, and God spoke to Job out of the storm. The answer to Job's problems was not an *explanation about God*, such as the three friends and Elihu had given, but a *revelation of God*. The four men had declared and defended the greatness of God but had failed to persuade Job. When God displayed His majesty and greatness, it humbled Job and brought him to the place of silent submission before God. That was the turning point.

Swiss psychologist Dr. Paul Tournier wrote in his book *Guilt and Grace* (Harper & Row, p. 86), "For God's answer is not an idea, a proposition, like the conclusion of a theorem; it is Himself. He revealed Himself to Job; Job found personal contact with God."

We prefer that God speak to us in the sunshine, but sometimes He must speak out of the storm. This is how He spoke to Israel on Mount Sinai (Ex. 19:16-19; Heb. 12:18) and centuries later to Elijah (1 Kings 19:8-11). Ezekiel saw the glory of God in a storm and heard the voice of God speaking to him (Ezek. 1–2). Experiencing this majestic demonstration of God's power made Job very susceptible to the message God had for him.

God's address to Job centered on His works in nature and consisted of seventy-seven questions interspersed with divine commentary relating to the questions. The whole purpose of this interrogation was to make Job realize his own inadequacy and inability to meet God *as an equal* and defend his cause.

"Then summon me, and I will answer," Job had challenged God, "or let me speak, and You reply" (Job 13:22, NIV). God had now responded to Job's challenge.

God's address can be summarized in three questions:

1. "Can you explain My creation?" (38:1-38)
2. "Can you oversee My creation?" (38:39–39:30)
Job's first response (40:1-5)
3. "Can you subdue My creation?" (40:6–41:34)
Job's second response (42:1-6)

The first question dealt with God's power and wisdom in bringing the universe into being. The second dealt with His providential care of His creatures, and the third centered on two creatures (probably the hippopotamus and the crocodile) that defy man's ability to subdue them. When Job repented of his self-righteousness, God restored him (vv. 7-17).

God is now called "the Lord," that is, Jehovah God, a name that (except for 12:9) has not been used in the Book of Job since the first two chapters. In their speeches, the men have called Him "God" and "the Almighty" but not "Jehovah." This is the name that God revealed to Israel centuries later (Ex. 3:13ff), the name that speaks of His self-existence ("I AM THAT I AM") and His personal covenant relationship to His people.

1. "Can you explain My creation?" (Job 38:1-38)
Job was sure that his speeches had been filled with wisdom and knowledge, but God's first question put an end to that

delusion: "Who is this that darkens My counsel with words without knowledge?" (Job 38:2, NIV) *The Living Bible* paraphrases it, "Why are you using your ignorance to deny My providence?" (TLB) God didn't question Job's integrity or sincerity; He only questioned Job's ability to explain the ways of God in the world. Job had spoken the truth about God (42:7), but his speeches had lacked humility. Job thought he knew about God, but he didn't realize how much he *didn't* know about God. Knowledge of our own ignorance is the first step toward true wisdom.

God began with *the Creation of the earth* (38:4-7) and compared Himself to a builder who surveys the site, marks off the dimensions, pours the footings, lays the cornerstone, and erects the structure. Creation was so wonderful that the stars sang in chorus and the angels (1:6; 2:1) shouted for joy, *but Job wasn't on the scene!* Then, how can he claim to know so much about the works of God?

From the beginning, God planned His Creation to be a garden of joyful beauty; but sin has turned Creation into a battlefield of ugliness and misery. Man in his selfishness is wasting natural resources, polluting land, air, water, and outer space, and so ravaging God's Creation that scientists wonder how long our planet will support life as we know it. Mahatma Gandhi was right: "There is a sufficiency in the world for man's need but not for man's greed."

The Lord then moved to a consideration of *the seas* (38:8-11). The image here is not *building* but *birth:* The seas were "knit together" in secret (v. 8; see Ps. 139:13) and then burst forth like a baby emerging from the womb. They were clothed with clouds and darkness, and their limits were set by God. "Who did all of this?" asked God of Job, and Job knew the answer.

The next aspect of Creation that God mentioned was *the sun* (Job 38:12-15). Here God pictured Himself as a general commanding His troops (the heavenly host). Had Job ever told the sun to rise and dispel the darkness? As the light spreads across the world, it reveals the details of the landscape, like the impression of a seal on clay or the unfolding of a beautiful garment taken out of a dark closet. But the light also puts an end to the evil deeds done in the darkness (John 3:19-21) and stops the criminal from attacking his victim.

The next eleven questions (Job 38:16-24) relate to the *vast dimensions of creation*. The average child today knows more about the heights and depths of the universe than Job and his friends could ever have imagined. Had Job ever taken a walk in the depths of the sea and visited "the gates of Sheol"? Did he know how far down he had to go to find the ocean's floor? (The greatest depth measured so far is in the Pacific Ocean— 35,810 feet or 6.78 miles.) And as for the reaches of space, *Voyager 2* spent twelve years going 4.4 billion miles, and in 1989 passed within 3,000 miles of Neptune's cloud bank!

In verses 19-21, God asked Job if he could calculate the reaches of east and west, or if the horizons were too much for him to measure. Then God inquired if Job understood the heights where the snow and hail were stored until God needed them (vv. 22-23; Ex. 9:18-26; Josh. 10:11) or the places where God kept His lightning and winds (Job 38:24). To be sure, God's words are full of irony; but that's what Job needed to puncture his pride and bring him to his knees in repentance.

How much did Job know about *the rain?* (vv. 25-28) Did he know how to plot its course so that it would accomplish God's purposes? Could he tell the lightning where and when to flash? Was he able to "father" rain and dew so that the land would have the water that it needed? Can he explain why God sends rain to the places where nobody lives? Then God turned from the spring and autumn rains to the winter *hail and frost* (vv. 29-30). If Job didn't know how the rain was "fathered," did he understand how the ice was "born"?

By this time, Job was probably wishing for a reprieve; but the Lord kept right on. He centered Job's attention on the heavens—the Pleiades, Orion the hunter, the various constellations ("Mazzaroth," KJV), and the Bear ("Arcturus" with his cubs). Did Job understand the laws that governed their movements, and could he control these stars and planets and make them appear in their proper seasons? Man may study the heavens, but he can't control them.

The question "Canst thou set its dominion in the earth?" (v. 33) is translated in the NASB, "Or fix their rule over the earth?" The NIV reads, "Can you set up God's dominion over the earth?" and The Living Bible says, "Do you know . . . how the heavens influence the earth?" Is there a suggestion here that the stars and planets have a direct influence over events on earth as the advocates of astrology maintain? Not at all. The statement can be paraphrased: "Job, if you understand so much about the heavenly bodies that are thought by some to affect the earth, then why don't you use that authority to change your situation?" The Lord was speaking with "holy sarcasm" and not revealing some profound truth.

In verses 34–38, the Lord called Job's attention to the clouds. Since Job knew the laws of the heavens, could he order the clouds to give rain? Was the lightning his servant, reporting for duty? Could Job take inventory of the clouds and "tip them over" like jars to make the rain come?

Creating all these things is one thing; maintaining them for man's good is quite something else. The Lord moved next into a series of questions about His providential working in the world. He moved from the inanimate world to the animate.

2. "Can you oversee My creation?" (Job 38:39–39:30)
The Lord brought before Job's imagination a parade of six beasts (lioness, goat, hind [deer], wild donkey, wild ox, and

horse) and five birds (raven, ostrich, stork, hawk, and eagle). As he contemplated these creatures, Job had to answer the question, "Do you understand how they live and how to take care of them?" Obviously, Job's reply had to be no.

The providence of God is certainly remarkable (see Ps. 104). In His wisdom and power, God supervises the whole universe and makes sure that His creatures are cared for. "You open Your hand and satisfy the desire of every living thing" (Ps. 145:16, NKJV). We humans have a difficult time keeping the machinery of life operating successfully, but God runs the whole universe with such precision that we build our scientific laws on His creation.

Did Job know how to feed the lion cubs or the young ravens? (Job 38:39-41) Would he even know that they were hungry? Where could he find food for them? The ravens would know to find the carcasses left behind by the lions because God taught the birds (even unclean ravens!) how to find food.

God then moved from the topic of death to the subject of birth. Did Job know the gestation periods for the goats and deer and how the young are born? (39:1-4) How do the little ones grow up safely, and how does the mother know when they are ready to leave home? Shepherds and farmers assist their animals during pregnancy and birth, but the wild beasts bring forth their young alone.

The wild donkey (vv. 5-8), also known as the *onager*, roamed the wilderness freely and refused to be domesticated. It survived without human assistance because God taught it how to take care of itself. The wild ox (the *aurochs*) was another "loner" in the animal kingdom (vv. 9-12), refusing to yield to the authority of men. You couldn't keep him in your barn, harness him to your plow, or force him to do your threshing.

"Now, Job," asked the Lord, "if you can't succeed with

these animals, how do you expect to succeed when you meet Me in court? How strong do you think you are?"

God then turned to a description of two birds, the stork ("peacock," KJV) and the ostrich (vv. 13-18). God asked Job no questions in this paragraph; He simply reminded him of the bizarre anatomy and behavior of the ostrich and suggested that perhaps Job could explain it.

The stork has beautiful wings that are very serviceable, but all the ostrich can do with her wings is fan the air! Why did God make a bird that couldn't fly but that could run faster than a horse? Why did He make a bird that puts her nest in such a vulnerable place where her eggs might be destroyed or eaten by a predator? Unlike most birds, why does she seem to be unmindful of her young?

The horse was next in line (vv. 19-25), an animal that was greatly admired and valued for strength and courage. This is a description of a war horse, not a farm horse; and you can visualize it prancing and pawing and eager to rush into the battle. When he hears the trumpet, he can't stand still, but runs so fast that he seems to be "eating up the ground." It was God, not Job, who made the horse with the strength and ability it needed to face danger and serve effectively on the field of battle.

The parade ended with two birds, the hawk and the eagle (vv. 26-30). Who gave the birds the instinct to migrate and the knowledge to build nests? Not Job! Eagles build their nests high on the cliffs; but God gave them keen eyesight so they can see their prey from afar, swoop down, and capture it. Eagles can also find corpses on which to feed themselves and their young because God made them that way.

3. Job's first response (Job 40:1-5)

God uses language that reflected Job's desire to take God to court and argue his case. "Will the faultfinder contend with the Almighty? Let him who reproves God answer it" (Job 40:2, NASB). God presented His case; now He gave Job opportunity to present his case. But Job has no case to present! His first words were, "Behold, I am vile!" which means, "I am insignificant and unworthy. I have no right to debate with God." Job had told his friends to cover their mouths (21:5), and others had covered their mouths when Job appeared (29:9); but now Job had to put his hand over his mouth lest he say something he shouldn't say (Prov. 30:32; Rom. 3:19). *Until we are silenced before God, He can't do for us what needs to be done.* As long as we defend ourselves and argue with God, He can't work for us and in us to accomplish His plan through us.

But Job was not quite broken and at the place of sincere repentance. He was silent but not yet submissive; so, God continued His address.

4. "Can you subdue My creation?" (Job 40:6–41:34)

Instead of confronting Job again with the broad sweep of His creation, God selected only two creatures and asked Job to consider them. It's as though God were saying, "My whole universe is too much for you to handle. However, here are two of My best products. What can you do with them?"

The issue now is not the *power* of God but the *justice* of God (Job 40:8). Job had said that God was unjust in the way He treated him (6:29; 27:1-6) and in the way He failed to judge the wicked (21:29-31; 24:1-17). In 40:9-14, God asked, "Job, do you have the strength and holy wrath it takes to judge sinners? If so, then start judging them! Humble the proud sinners and crush the wicked! Bury them! You claim that you can do a better job than I can of bringing justice to the world, so I'll let you do it!"

However, before God turned Job loose on the sinners of the world, He asked him to put on his majestic robes and "practice" on two of His finest creatures, the hippopotamus (vv. 15-24) and the crocodile (41:1-34). If Job succeeded in subduing them, then he would qualify to execute judgment against a sinful world.

The hippopotamus (Job 40:15-24). Most students agree that the animal described is the hippopotamus, although some prefer the elephant or the water buffalo. The word "behemoth" is the transliteration of a Hebrew word that means "super-beast." Today's big-game hunter with his modern weapons would probably not be deterred by the hippo's size or strength, but this beast was a formidable enemy in the days of arrows and spears.

God reminded Job that He was the Creator of both the hippo and man (v. 15), and yet He made them different. The hippo eats grass and is strong and mighty; Job ate a variety of fine foods and was weak and unable to fight with the hippo. The hippo has a powerful body, with strong muscles and bones like iron rods; while man's body is (comparatively speaking) weak and easily damaged. The hippo lounges in the river, hidden under the water, and feeds on the vegetation that washes down from the hills; while man has to toil to earn his daily bread. A raging river doesn't frighten the hippo, and hunters don't alarm him. In Job's day, it was next to impossible to capture the hippopotamus; but how easy it is to capture a man!

"Now, Job," asks the Lord, "can you capture and subdue this great creature? If so, then I'll believe that you have the power and wisdom to judge the world justly."

The crocodile (Job 41:1-34). The word "leviathan" is the transliteration of a Hebrew word, the root of which means "to twist, to writhe." People used the word to describe the "sea monsters" that were supposed to inhabit the Mediterranean. Psalm 104:25-26 may refer to whales or dolphins. The Jews used the word to describe their enemies (Isa. 27:1), especially Egypt (Ps. 74:13-14). Revelation 12:9 refers to Satan as "that old serpent." In mythology, the leviathan was a many-headed monster that ruled the waters and feared no man.

"Can you capture the leviathan?" asked the Lord. "And if you can, what will you do with him?" (see Job 41:1-11) Well, what can you do with a captured crocodile? You can't make a pet out of him, no matter how agreeable he seems to be (vv. 3-5); and the merchants won't want to buy him from you (v. 6). If you try to train him, you'll quit in a hurry and never try to do it again! (vv. 8-9) God drew a practical conclusion: "If you can't come to grips with the crocodile, how will you ever be able to stand before Me?" (vv. 10-11)

In verses 12-24, God gave a poetical description of this great creature's mighty limbs, fierce teeth and strong jaws, and impregnable covering (vv. 12-17). When the crocodile churns up the river and blows out water, the sun reflects from the vapor; and it looks like fire and smoke from a dragon's mouth (vv. 18-21). His armor is so strong that he can go anywhere without fear (vv. 22-24).

The chapter closes with a description of the leviathan's anger and courage (vv. 25-34). People flee from him in fear (v. 25), but he doesn't flee from them. In verses 26-29, God named eight different weapons that the leviathan laughs at and treats like pieces of straw or rotten wood. Just as this creature fears nothing *around* him, so he fears nothing *under* him; for his underside is protected with a covering like sharp pieces of pottery (v. 30). He fears no enemy on the land or in the water (vv. 31-32), for he makes the water to foam like the ingredients in the apothecary's mixing pot. And when he swims through the water, the wake looks like the white hair of an old man!

5. Job's second response (Job 42:1-6)
Job knew he was beaten. There was no way he could argue his case with God. Quoting God's very words (Job 42:3-4),

Job humbled himself before the Lord and acknowledged His power and justice in executing His plans (v. 2). Then Job admitted that his words had been wrong and that he had spoken about things he didn't understand (v. 3). Job withdrew his accusations that God was unjust and not treating him fairly. He realized that whatever God does is right and man must accept it by faith.

Job told God, "I can't answer Your questions! All I can do is confess my pride, humble myself, and repent." Until now, Job's knowledge of God had been indirect and impersonal; but that was changed. Job had met God personally and seen himself to be but "dust and ashes" (v. 6; 2:8, 12; Gen. 18:27).

"The door of repentance opens into the hall of joy," said Charles Spurgeon; and it was true for Job. In the climax of the book, Job *the sinner* became Job *the servant of God* (Job 42:7-9). Four times in these verses God called Job by that special Old Testament title "My servant" (see 1:8; 2:3). How did Job serve God? By enduring suffering and not cursing God, and thereby silencing the devil! Suffering in the will of God is a ministry that God gives to a chosen few.

But Job the servant became Job *the intercessor.* God was angry with Job's three friends because they hadn't told the truth about Him (42:7), and they had to be reconciled to Job so he could pray for them. *Job became the umpire between God and his three friends!* By forgiving his friends and praying for them, Job brought back the blessing to his own life (v. 10). We only hurt ourselves when we refuse to forgive others.

Job ended up with twice as much as he had before. He had twenty children, ten with God and ten in his home. (He and his wife were also reunited.) Friends and relatives brought money for a "restoration fund," which Job must have used for purchasing breeders; and eventually, Job had twice as much livestock as before. He was once again a wealthy man. If the "double" formula also applied to Job's age, then he must have been seventy when the story began (Ps. 90:10), and God allowed Job to live twice as many years (Job 42:16).

In the East, parents are especially proud of beautiful daughters, and Job had three of them: Jemimah ("dove"), Keziah ("cinnamon") and Keren-Happuch ("horn of eye paint"). Jemimah had quietness, Keziah had perfume, and Keren-Happuch had the cosmetics!

To die "old and full of years" was the goal of every person. It means more than a long life; it means a rich and full life that ends well. This is the way Abraham and Isaac died (Gen. 25:8; 35:29), and also King David (1 Chron. 29:28).

POSTLUDE

We must not misinterpret this final chapter and conclude that every trial will end with all problems solved, all hard feelings forgiven, and everybody "living happily ever after." It just doesn't always happen that way! This chapter assures us that, no matter what happens to us, *God always writes the last chapter.* Therefore, we don't have to be afraid. We can trust God to do what is right, no matter how painful our situation might be.

But Job's greatest blessing was not the regaining of his health and wealth or the rebuilding of his family and circle of friends. His greatest blessing was *knowing God better and understanding His working in a deeper way.* As James wrote, "You have heard of the perseverance of Job and seen the purpose of the Lord, that the Lord is very compassionate and merciful" (James 5:11, NKJV). And Hebrews 12:11 reminds us: "Now, no chastening seems to be joyous for the present, but grievous; nevertheless, afterward it yields the peaceable fruit of righteousness to those who have been trained by it" (NKJV).

"In the whole story of Job," wrote G. Campbell Morgan, "we see the patience of God and endurance of man. When these act in fellowship, the issue is certain. It is that of the coming forth from the fire as gold, that of receiving the crown of life" *(The Answers of Jesus to Job,* Baker, p. 117).

No matter what God permits to come into our lives, He always has His "afterward." He writes the last chapter—and that makes it worth it all.

Therefore, BE PATIENT!